For my cousin,
John Saunders

THE HISTORY OF FERNHILL HEATH
The Village of North Claines

Copyright © Gill Lawley 2007.

All rights reserved. No part of this publication may be reproduced, stored in a retrieval system, or transmitted, in any form or by any means, electronic, mechanical, photocopying, recording or otherwise, without the prior permission in writing of the publisher.

ISBN 978-0-9557899-0-8

Published by:
Sunnyside Publishing
49 Station Road
Fernhill Heath
Worcester
WR3 7UJ

Printed and bound in the United Kingdom 9 8 7 6 5 4 3 2 1

Printed by:
Double.p Print Ltd
7-9 Beoley Road West
St. Georges
Redditch
Worcestershire
B98 8LR

By the same author:
'Of the Parish Here and There' - *The History of Martin Hussingtree.*

THE HISTORY OF FERNHILL HEATH
The Village of North Claines

Gill Lawley

ACKNOWLEDGEMENTS

The author would like to thank the following for their assistance -

Archdiocese of Birmingham, Jim Berry, Birmingham City Archives, Ken Bray, Phyllis Byatt, the late Doris Chance, Claines Church, Derry & Gwen Clifford, the late Colin Cook, Evening News, Brian & Norma Haden, Mr. & Mrs. J. Harwood, Hindlip CE First School, Mrs. Lane and the late Dick Lane, Don Lawley, Roy & Bronwyn Mitchell, Morton House Nursing & Rest Home, Susan Nixon, North Claines Parish Council, Dorothy Owen, Tony & Lou Palmer, Ruth Piggott, Alan Richards, The River School, Valerie Rosendorff, John Saunders, Mr. & Mrs. A. Thomson, Bill Toppin, Eileen Wiggin, Eileen Williams, Worcestershire Library and History Centre and Worcestershire Record Office. Mike Wall for proof-reading.

MAPS

The National Archives, Ordnance Survey and Worcestershire Record Office.

PHOTOGRAPHS

Brenda Baylis, Phylis Byatt, Derry & Gwen Clifford, Joyce Eden, Evening News, Fred Hickman, Hindlip C. E. First School, Graham Lawley, Dr. Malcolm Nixon, Bob & Joan Rosier and The River School.

Photographs taken by Mrs. W. R. Young, B. Buckle and the County Surveyor are part of the Worcestershire Photographic Survey deposited at Worcestershire Record Office.

CHAPTERS

I.	Introduction	VI
1.	Claines	1
2.	Vernal Heath - A Settlement	11
3.	From a Settlement to a Village	25
4.	1900-1950	41
5.	1951-2000	67
6.	The Workhouse	81
7.	Hindlip School	93
8.	From Rose Bank to Sandyway	105
	Image References	157
	Index	161

INTRODUCTION

I began my research for this book in 2000 and very slowly uncovered a unique and complex history of Fernhill Heath.

The first chapter opens with a broad overview of Fernhill Heath within the manor and parish of Claines. The next four chapters span, in chronological order, the period from 1700 - 2000 of an in-depth look at the gradual development of Fernhill Heath from a settlement to a village. I decided to start at 1700 because a few years into the century the Droitwich Road became a Turnpike with various Acts. In the mid 18th century there were a few cottages, an inn and two farms in the village and several scattered around the edge. By the end of that century it was still only sparsely inhabited. The growth of Fernhill Heath began a few years after the opening of a workhouse on the Droitwich Road in 1813. By 1841 the village had grown to some 90 houses alongside and behind the Droitwich Road, and by 1901 had almost doubled in size. There were no houses built during World War I and building began in the mid to late 1920s. The first housing development was built in the 1930s. After World War II house building began again and the village continued to expand up to 2000.

Some land and ownership have been difficult to identify. Farms have been sold, split up and parcels of land exchanged. Cottages built in the 18th and 19th centuries had a lifespan of about 80 years, those that did last longer, were gradually pulled down as unfit for habitation, very few are still standing.

Moving in and out of these four chapters are other relevant topics relating to the history of Fernhill Heath. The Manorial Courts, Church records, the Hindlip Estate, the railway, the Droitwich Road and M5 motorway. The two World Wars are briefly touched upon. There have been contentious issues; speed limits, a water and sewage scheme, the history of the recreation ground, a proposed replacement Hindlip School and further housing expansion.

The sixth and seventh chapters cover the history of the workhouse and Hindlip School. The last chapter is a compilation of the history of some of the houses built during the 18th and 19th centuries and other properties in the 20th century.

Note: Prior to 1883 the village name was spelt 'Vernal Heath' and 'Fearnall Heath', and these spellings have been used during the appropriate period. The same applies to several localities within and around the village that are not in general usage today, i.e. The Widefield, Links Lane, Red Hill, Puck Pit Farm/Pulpit Farm, Deans Green Farm, otherwise The Wheatfield, Station Road, Rose Bank, The Grange and Danes Green Farm.

Chapter 1
Claines

Fernhill Heath lies 3 miles north of Worcester on the A38 road to Droitwich, beginning at the A449 Northern Link road bridge crossing the A38 on Rose Bank to Hindlip Lodge a distance of 1¼ miles, and from east to west about the same distance.

The main road through Fernhill Heath is pre-Roman and was part of an old salt track later called the Lower Saltway that came down from Droitwich to Worcester to where it joined Salt Lane (Castle Street) and continued down to the River Severn.[1] During the Roman occupation AD.43–AD.410 the Romans re-routed the Lower Saltway at Sandyway, north of Fernhill Heath, and cut across the lower part of, what was later to become Hindlip Park, to Spellis, onto Rainbow Hill and down into Lowesmoor, Worcester. This road was later abandoned as a Saltway because the heavy clay soil in some places made it extremely difficult for the packhorses to travel, although it stayed in use across Hindlip Park as a local track until 1828 when it was closed to carts and redefined as a footpath.[2]

When ecclesiastical parish boundaries were laid down the old Roman road across Hindlip Park to Spellis was used to separate the parishes of Hindlip and Claines. The Martin Brook at Sandyway was the meeting point of the three parishes of Martin Hussingtree, Hindlip and Claines.

In 1944 Worcester City Council commissioned an outline plan for the development and enhancement of the City and County. With the likelihood of an increase in traffic from Droitwich to Worcester, a recommendation was put forward that the ¾ mile stretch of Roman road between Sandyway and Spellis should be rebuilt, bypassing Fernhill Heath and continuing southwards down Blackpole Road towards Worcester.[3] Neither this recommendation nor a similar one put forward by Wychavon District Council in 1985 were taken up.

At Sandyway another Roman track called the Green Weg or Green Way,

---

[1] *The Ancient Highways and Tracks of Worcestershire and the Middle Severn Basin. Part I, II, III.* G. B. Grundy.
[2] *WRO. Quarter Sessions. Michaelmas 1828. Vol. II. Fol. 419 & 420.*
[3] *An Outline Development Plan for the County of the City of Worcester.* Minoprio & Spencely, FFRIBA, AAMTPI. 1946.

later Green Lane, ran in an easterly direction onto the Pershore Lane and up to Oddingley. In 1864 Green Lane was closed to carts, re-routed, and defined as a footpath.[4]

The hill ridge to the west of Rose Bank on which Oakfield House (The River School) stands was a toot-hill; a look-out post, and the site of a Roman signalling camp situated between Elbury Hill ½ mile east of Worcester and Ombersley to the northwest, communication was by means of beacons. Toot-hill was gradually corrupted to Tootenhall or Tetnal and now Tutnall; Tutnall House is in Claines Lane, Claines.

The present spelling of 'Fernhill Heath' was adopted in 1883.[5] Two explanations have been suggested as to why the name was changed from 'Fearnall Heath'. Firstly, several years after the opening in 1852 of the Oxford, Worcester and Wolverhampton Railway all trains to Worcester halted at Fearnall Heath station for tickets to be checked and the local wits began calling the village 'Infernal Heath'! To stop the witticisms the name was tidied up to 'Fernhill Heath' and the railway company, by then the Great Western, was gradually persuaded to adopt it.[6] Secondly, the 1st Lady Hindlip took a dislike to the name 'Fearnall Heath' and it came to be called 'Fernhill Heath'. In 1956 a North Claines Parish Councillor proposed a resolution to change the present name back to the 18th century spelling, 'Vernal Heath', declaring, "Fernhill Heath hasn't got a hill or any fern and there is something attractive about Vernal. Fernhill Heath is merely a postal address." The resolution was later withdrawn.[7] Local residents who were born and bred here pronounce the village as 'Fearnall Heath' whilst newcomers stress the second syllable of the first word as Fernhill Heath.

Before the change to Fernhill Heath its name had been written variously as Fournall (12th cent), Fernhull (13th and 14th cent), Ffournall (17th cent), Fernhull, Vernal and Vernals (18th cent), Vernal, Fearnal, Fearnall, Fernal and Fernhill (19th cent). Some of the field names reveal that the area had once been rough moorland; The Moors, Heather Moor, Dillmoor, Ling Meadow, The Broom, Sugar and Seg Mead. Small wooded areas lay to the east and west, Woodfields, The Hurst, Otter Hurst and Stubby

---

[4] *WRO. BA 2164.*
[5] *Claines Church Parish Registers.*
[6] *Berrow's Worcester Journal. Worcestershire Villages by 'A Stroller'.*
[7] *WRO. BA 10533/2.*

Furlong, and scattered Perry Crofts. The geology of the area indicates that Fernhill Heath lies on gravel beds below Triassic Keuper Marl. There are five Terraces sloping down from Martin Hussingtree to the Flood Plain beyond Worcester Cathedral, and Fernhill Heath lies on Terrace 4. Sandyway, as the name implies, is a particularly sandy area stretching from the northern boundary across the lower part of Hindlip Park to the village, and across to the east side of Station Road. There are a number of exhausted clay pits on the west side of Station Road, in Hurst Lane and in the grounds of Oakfield House.

Anciently Fernhill Heath was in the tithing of Tapenhall, a name synonymous today with Tapenhall Road, Tapenhall House, Tapenhall and Upper Tapenhall Farms. The name 'Tapenhall' was derived from 'Tapen halan', meaning 'The nook of Tapa'. A 'nook' was a triangular meadow or field, and 'Tapa' an Anglo Saxon personal name. In the time of Lyfing, Bishop of Worcester, a charter dated 1038 granted two hides of land, approximately 240 acres, in Tapan halan (Tapenhall) to a certain Earcytel for three lives with reversion to the Bishop of Worcester. Some of its boundaries do not coincide with existing boundaries and some of the landmarks mentioned in the charter are difficult to ascertain.

The boundary began north at the Broad Ford the boundary brook with Martin Hussingtree, fording the highway at Sandyway, and in an easterly direction turned onto the Roman road and across Hindlip Park where it turned south westwards to the grove (near Hurst Cottage in Hurst Lane), and continued onto a bridle path into Port Straet (Worcester-Droitwich Road) then turned southwest towards Dillmoor (Dilmore), then westwards to where the stream or springs rise nearby (The Grange). Along the sandy road to the Bishop's piece of land (southeast of the grounds of Hawford House) the boundary continued to Linacres Farm. Though this brought the boundary near to the River Salwarpe four landmarks are unidentified before the river is reached, and it is probable that the boundary reached the River Salwarpe near Mildenham Mill. Here the boundary most likely crossed the river and met the stream that comes down from the north and passes just east of Chatley to join the Salwarpe at Mildenham Mill, this would have included the northernmost Tapenhall Farm in Ombersley. The boundary followed the course of the River Salwarpe to Tapenhall Mill (Porters Mill) at the point where the Martin Brook runs into the river, the

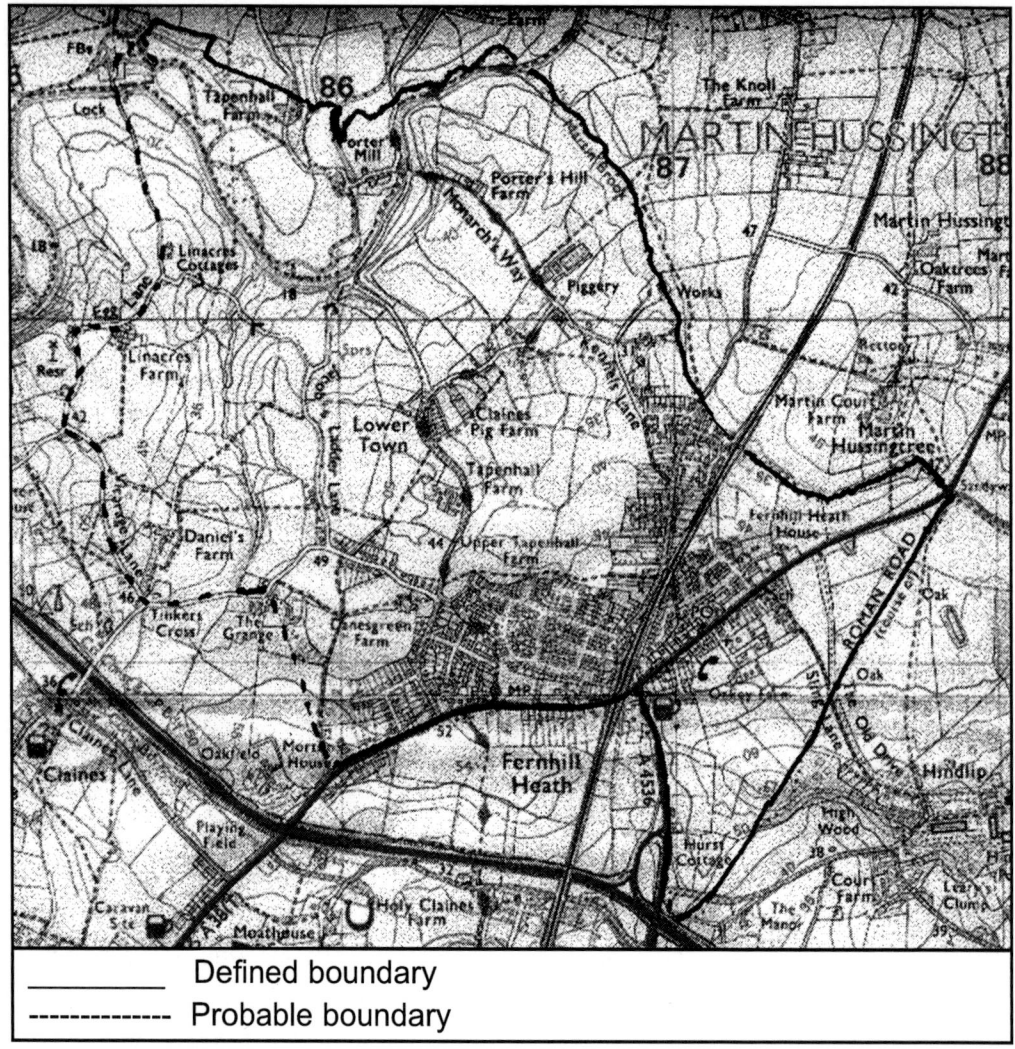

Defined boundary
---------- Probable boundary

Fig 1. Map of Tapenhall.   Scale 1:50 000

brook formed the northwest and north boundaries leading back to the Broad Ford (Martin Brook) at Sandyway.[8]

At some early time the Mull/Mulls family were the most important inhabitants of Tapenhall. Later the Porter family inherited, and one John Porter, an eminent lawyer, was macebearer to Elizabeth I and churchwarden at Claines Church. On or about the 15th August 1575, Elizabeth I, with a great retinue, paid a visit to John Porter's home (Porters Mill Hall) on her way to Worcester. The Porter family became extinct in 1709 on the death of George Porter who died childless. Porters Mill Hall was the principal house in Tapenhall.

---

[8] *Saxon Charters of Worcestershire. G. B. Grundy. 1929.*

Tapenhall was one of nine tithings or hamlets in the manor of Northwick; Whistones (now The Tything), Beverburn (now Barbourne), Hollow or Holy Claines, Astwood, Bevereye (now Bevere), Tollerdine or Tolwardine (now Tolladine), Milnham with Hayford (now Mildenham with Hawford) and Smite (now in the parish of Hindlip).

Northwick may have dated back to 680 when the Diocese of Worcester was founded. Claines at that time was the name of only a small area in the manor.

The first church at Claines, dedicated to St. John The Baptist, was built in 957 as a Chapel of Ease to St. Helen's, Worcester.

In 964, by a charter of King Edgar, the Hundred of Oswaldslow was formed, taking its name from Oswald the then Bishop of Worcester. The Hundred was a consolidation of three ancient Hundreds; Wulfereshaw, Winburge Tree and Cutherbergelaw, the object of which was to unite into one Hundred the great possessions of the Bishopric of Worcester and the monasteries connected with it. Northwick became part of the newly formed Hundred of Oswaldslow and was the principal rural manor lying near to the River Severn.

In 1085 King William sent commissioners throughout England to record the value of land, landowners, manors, hundreds and townships for taxation purposes. This record later became known as the Domesday Book of 1086. Northwick is recorded as containing 25 hides of land (a hide was 120 acres), 18 ploughs and 3 mills, Hawford, Mildenham and Tapenhall (Porters Mill). The manor owned 90 houses in Worcester and one salt-house in Droitwich.

In 1234 Claines became a separate parish with the Bishop of Worcester taking Claines and the Prior taking St. Helen's with land to the west of St. Helen's.[9] The present Claines church was erected about 1400 and restored in 1885.

The Lay Subsidy Rolls for the manor of Northwick in 1280 record freeholders paying a subsidy or tax to the King, amongst whom were; de Willielmo de Fernhull, de Matilda de Fernhull, de Johanne de Totenhulle, and in 1332-33 de Johanne de Fernhull, de Johanne de Totenhall, and de Roberto de Mildenham.

---

[9] *Worcestershire Nuggets. Page 91. John Noake. 1889.*

Over the centuries the importance of the manor of Northwick diminished, and in 1648 the manor house was sold into private hands. In the same year the manor was confiscated and sold, but on the accession of Charles II in 1660 was returned to the Bishop with its title changed to Whistones, and soon afterwards altered to Claines and Whistones. Claines later superseded the title of Claines and Whistones.

The manor of Claines, 7 miles in circumference, commenced north at Sandyway, across Hindlip Park, separating the parish from Hindlip but taking in Smite, bounded by Warndon to Lyppards Farm but excluding the farm itself, to Worcester to St. Martin's Gate and then to the Foregate, to the Liberty Post at the top of Salt Lane (Castle Street), westwards down to the River Severn, up the middle of the river to Hawford, along the River Salwarpe to Tapenhall Mill (Porters Mill), picking up Martin Brook and back along the brook to Sandyway.

Manorial Courts were the civil government of the day and frequently held to enforce its customs and fining all leaseholders and copyholders who did not attend the Court Barons. The Steward, Parish Constables, Haywards and Overseers of the Highway were appointed at these Courts. The Bishopric's ownership of the manor of Claines lasted some twelve centuries and finally ended in 1860 with its transfer to the Ecclesiastical Commissioners.

From Tudor times in the 16th century until the late 19th century Claines Church through its Vestry collected local rates, appointed Churchwardens and Overseers of the Poor. The church administered charities and still does so today with the Claines United Charity. Claines was an 'Open Vestry' allowing all male ratepayers to attend and vote. In 1821 under the Sturges Bourne Act of 1819 the parish established a 'Select Vestry' that enacted voting on a scale relating to land ownership, 20 members were appointed but this was later reduced to 13, that coincidently would be the same number appointed with the formation of the civil Parish Council in 1894.

Several Acts of Parliament relating to the poor in the 18th and early 19th centuries brought about the opening of a workhouse in Fearnall Heath in 1813 and which finally closed in 1838 following the introduction of the Poor Law Amendment Act of 1834. The opening of the workhouse led indirectly to the development of the village.

In 1830 a new church in Barbourne was built, St. George's, a Chapel of Ease to Claines Church.

The continuing rise in the population of Worcester led to the 'carving up' of the manor and parish of Claines with several boundary extensions moving northwards out of the city. In 1832 the boundary was moved to The Tything and in 1835 to Barbourne Brook. In 1862 the parish of St. George's was founded, and the old church built in 1830 was demolished and the present church built in 1894. More new parishes followed; St. Stephen's also in 1862, St. Mary Magdalene in the Arboretum 1877-1977, St. Barnabas at Rainbow Hill in 1883, and in the 20th century, Christ Church at Tolladine (Chapel of Ease) 1947.[10]

The city boundary was again extended in 1867 and land to the north was taken into the city as far as Bilford Road, Checketts Lane and part of Northwick. Under the Worcester Extension Act of 1885 Claines was split into two parts. The earlier 1867 city extension into Claines became known as South Claines. North of this new boundary was the county part of Claines or North Claines of which the remainder of Northwick, and the now defunct tithings of Holy Claines, Astwood, Bevere, Tolladine, Mildenham with Hawford, Smite and Tapenhall were included.

Claines National School opened in 1841 and Hindlip School at Sandyway in 1869.

In 1879 a Mission Room or Chapel of Ease was erected at Fearnall Heath for the use of parishioners to save them walking to Claines Church. The following year by the Divided Parishes Act, Upper Smite in Claines was moved into Hindlip and Lower Smite brought into Claines from Warndon parish.

Under the Local Government Act of 1888 the Worcestershire County Council was set up. A further Act in 1894 introduced civil parish councils and the Parish Council of North Claines was formed in the same year to deal with matters at a local level and as a rural parish came under the umbrella of the Droitwich Rural District Council at which one parish representative was returned, this was later increased to two in 1926.

Under the Pluralities Act of 1838 the ecclesiastical parish of Claines was altered at its northern end in 1895 when part of Fernhill Heath, Spellis and a detached part of Smite Hill were annexed to the parishes of Hindlip and

---

[10] *Old and New Parishes in the Worcester area.* Ruth Piggott. 1984.

Martin Hussingtree. Transferred to Hindlip was the eastern side of Fernhill Heath from Sandyway along the Droitwich Road past the railway bridge taking in and including three properties and a piece of land (now Stoneycroft Close), down to Spellis Fields and back along the old Roman road boundary.

Smite Farm and Smite Hill were adjoined to Martin Hussingtree. Also transferred from Claines to Martin Hussingtree was that part of Fernhill Heath commencing near the third milestone from Worcester in a northerly direction, turning west (between where Goodwood House and Heathside Hotel now stand), across certain pieces of land, (now Goodwood Close, east of Dilmore Avenue, east of Perrycroft Close, west of Station Road, to the top of Kennels Lane), along the northern boundary of land owned by the Worcestershire Hunt to Martin Brook following the brook to Sandyway and then proceeding in a south-westerly direction along the west side of the Droitwich Road back to near the third milestone.

Under this Act the burial of the dead in these two areas of Fernhill Heath was no longer permitted in Claines churchyard unless a husband or wife had already been interred there. Future interments took place at either Hindlip or Martin Hussingtree depending on where the resident had lived in Fernhill Heath. This later brought about a shortage of burial space in both churchyards, and in 1910 the 3rd Lord Hindlip gave a piece of land from Spellis Farm for a cemetery and a small chapel, and at Martin Hussingtree the lord of the manor, The Revd H. W. Hill, gave a portion of land to the southeast of the church in 1911 for interments.

In 1906 Worcester failed in their attempt to move the boundary northwards to Claines Lane that would have taken in Claines Church. Further expansion of Worcester occurred in 1931 when the remainder of Northwick, Perdiswell and part of Cornmeadow Lane were taken into the city. The boundary was altered at its eastern edge in 1948 when Astwood and Tolladine farms were moved into Warndon parish. In 1987 the present boundary was moved north to the A449 Northern Link Relief Road and part of Bevere was lost to Worcester city.

In 1974 under the reorganisation of local government the Worcestershire County Council merged with Herefordshire to become Hereford and Worcester County Council until 1998 when it reverted back to a unitary county council. Rural district councils were also abolished in 1974 and the three towns of Droitwich, Evesham and Pershore were amalgamated to

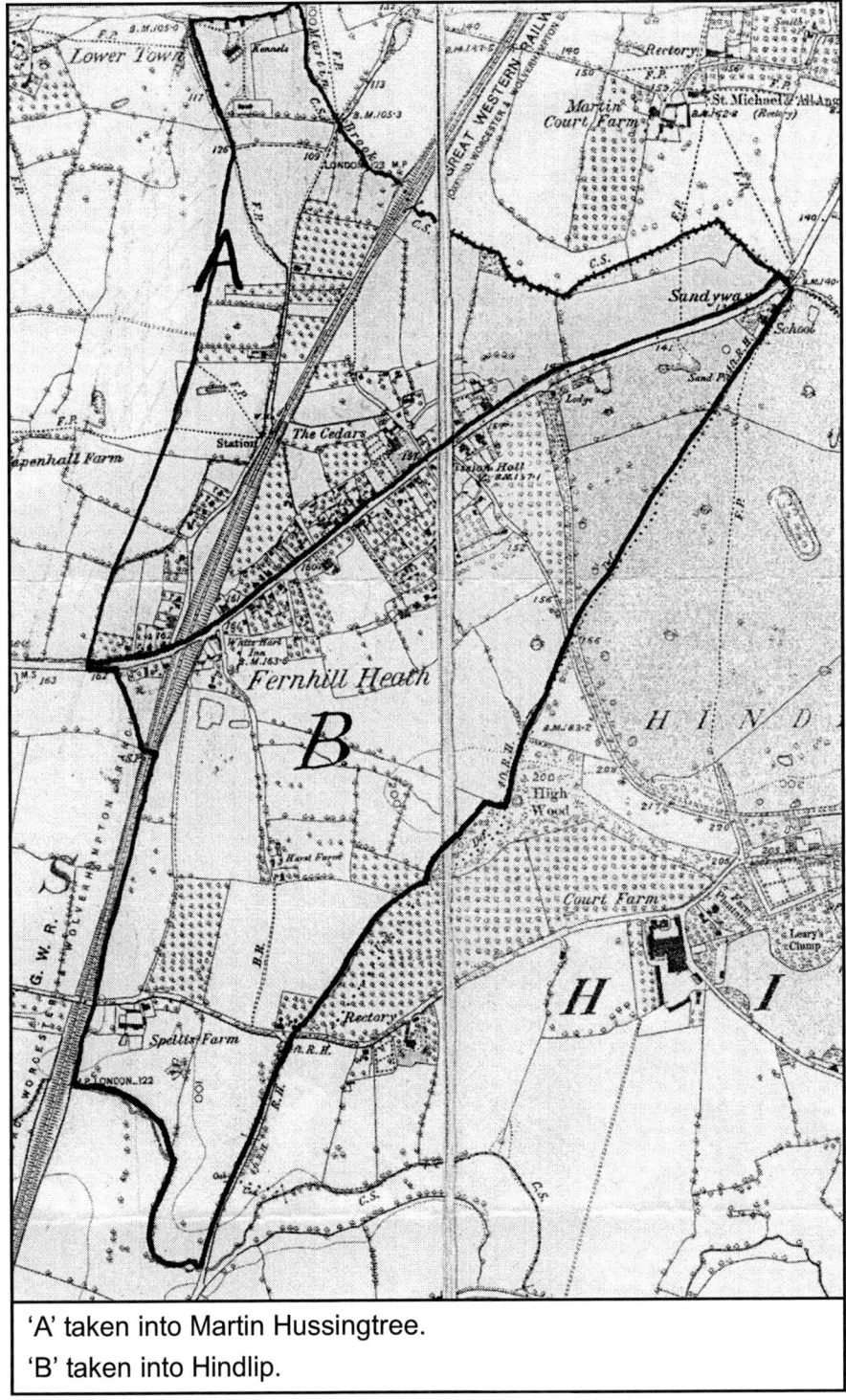

'A' taken into Martin Hussingtree.
'B' taken into Hindlip.

Fig 2. Ecclesiastical Parish boundaries 1895

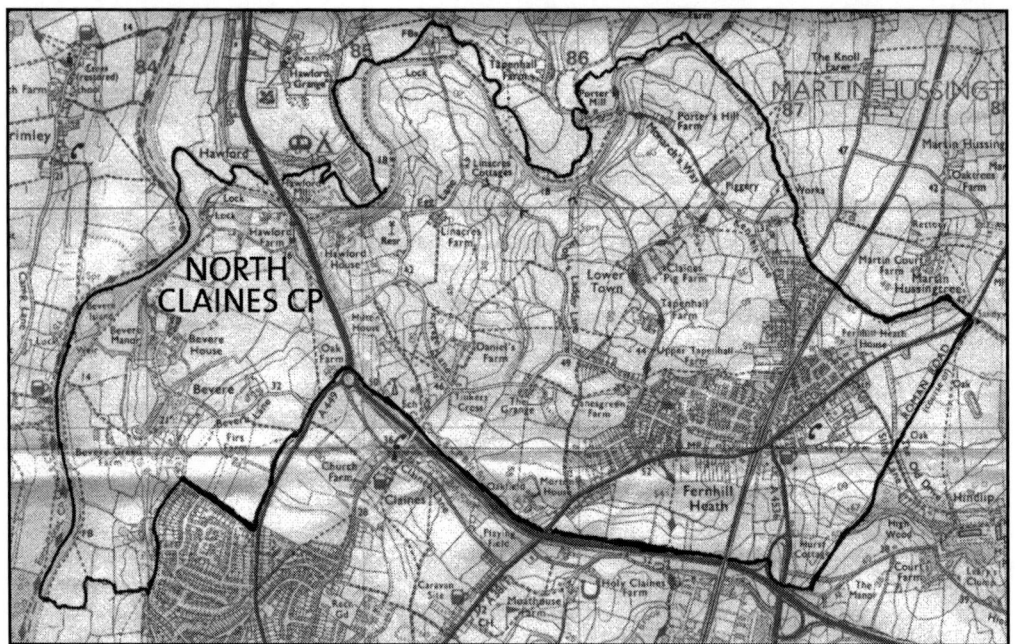

Fig 3. North Claines Civil Parish Boundary 1987. Scale 1:50 000

form Wychavon District Council and two parish councillors were again returned to represent North Claines ward on the newly formed District Council.

Chapter 2
Vernal Heath – A Settlement

Fernhill Heath in the early 18th century was a settlement consisting of a few farms and cottages on heath and moorland; Vernal Heath and Dillmoor (Dilmore). The narrow highway passing through Vernal Heath was known as the Wich Road and from the present-day Dilmore Lane to Rose Bank; Red Hill.

Wich Road

The highway from Worcester to Droitwich was a worn, dirt track in a dreadful condition for sometimes as much as nine months of the year, and in 1713 an Act of Parliament was passed to repair it between these two places. In June the following year the highway from Worcester via Droitwich to Bromsgrove became a Turnpike that lasted until 1869. A Turnpike Trust was set up with trustees, amongst others, representatives of every parish that the road passed through. Tolls were introduced to pay towards the maintenance of the road and in Barbourne a tollhouse was later built at the junction of the Droitwich and Ombersley Roads leading out of Worcester. A second Act passed in 1726 enabled the Turnpike Trust to take away gravel, stone and sand from the common land in any neighbouring parish, town, village or hamlet free of charge to repair the highway. Gravel was taken from the pits on Vernal Heath, several of which, spilt over onto the narrow highway creating a danger to travellers and the Manorial Courts ordered the Turnpike's Surveyor of the Highways to repair them.

In 1733 the inhabitants of Spellis Green were fined 10s.0d for not repairing the highway (Hindlip Lane) to the foot of Red Hill. The long haul up and down Red Hill was notoriously difficult for horses and carriages, carts and wains, and many incidents are recorded in the Manorial Court Rolls of reporting the bad state of Red Hill to the Turnpike Trust and the long delays before any improvements were made. The Highways Act of 1734 ordered all landowners adjacent to the highway to cut and keep the trees and hedges in order so that the sun and air could dry out the surface, prohibited them from starting fires within 80 feet of the middle of the road and to scour the ditches. The landowners were responsible for providing local labour and during harvest time no highway work was permitted within the parish. In 1749 another Act was passed giving Justices of the Peace the authority to determine the Statutory work to be carried out on the highway, this was abolished in 1835. In the same Act of 1749 highways were to be measured and milestones erected, one mile between them starting from Worcester Cross.

The Heath was open common or wasteland and stretched north to south from the present-day Sling Lane to Ivy Lane, and east to west from O'Keys Farm into Post Office Lane. All commoners had the right to graze their animals on the Heath, and at times there were several hundred sheep grazing and sometimes causing a nuisance to travellers who had to stop and remove them before passing on their way.

There were four tracks off the Wich Road. The first track or the present-day Post Office Lane is described later in this chapter under the sub heading, 'The Widefield and Perry-field'. The second track or the present-day Hurst Lane turned off the Wich Road to Hurst Farm and on to Spellis Green and Blackpole. The third track was Links Lane now the present-day Station Road. Links Lane was named after a small meadow on the west side of the lane. 'Links' was a corruption of the word 'Ling' a species of heather. Links Lane went down to Martin Brook, the parish boundary with Martin Hussingtree. On the other side of the brook was Stocking Lane leading to Ladywood and Salwarpe. The fourth track, later called Dilmore Lane, took its name from two fields on Red Hill; Dillmoor and Great Dillmoor, and led to Lower Town and Tapenhall Mill (Porters Mill).

Copyhold and Freehold land

In common with many landowners in the 18th century the Bishopric of Worcester commissioned an estate plan with a terrier of the Manor of Claines in 1751. Four landmarks, Vernal Heath, Red Hill, and two open copyhold fields, the Widefield and Perry-field identify Fernhill Heath.

There was very little freehold, mostly copyhold land. The copyhold tenants of the farms and cottages held their land by right of title from the lords of the manor. A copy of the lease was given to the tenant, hence the word 'copyholder'. The copyhold lease was granted for the lives of three named persons, but it might last in practice for four lives, because the widow of a male tenant dying in possession was allowed what is called 'free bench' so long as she remained unwed.

When transferring the copyhold by descent on the death of a tenant, upon the marriage of any widow or surrender, the new tenant paid a fine to the lord of the manor of a heriot, usually a beast, but this was later commuted to money. The copyholders' rent days were Lady Day 25th March and Michaelmas 29th September. Copyholders could buy out their leases, highly profitable sums to the lords of the manor. Copyhold tenancies were abolished in 1922.

The freeholders held their land without any conditions attached and could sell and let as they so wished.

Fig 4. Vernal Heath 1751-1753   Part of the Manor of Claines.   No. Scale.

There were very few cottages on the Heath. Only four on the east side of the Wich Road; two were in the vicinity of the present-day Ivy Lane and belonged to Spellis Farm, the other two, copyhold cottages, were situated on the south corner of the present-day Hurst Lane in 2 and 1 roods of garden, one occupied by John Farmer and the other by the poor of Clains (sic) respectively.

On the west side of the Wich Road were five copyhold cottages occupied by –

a.	John Lloyd	Cottage & garden		1 rood
b.	William Taylor	"	"	1 rood
c.	William Smith	"	"	2 roods
d.	Thomas Chance	"	"	1 rood
e.	William Hill	"	"	2 roods

A rood is an old measurement equalling ¼ of an acre. The annual rental for the cottages in 1753 was 1s.0d per annum irrespective of the size of the land or the cottage.

Around the edge of the Heath were several copyhold farms whose owners lived away and tenant farmers were put in to manage them.

To the north Sir William Compton of Hindlip House held 44 acres comprising on the east side from Sandyway, the Briary Fields or the lower part of Hindlip Park over which the carriage drive to Hindlip House passed, a bowling green, a blacksmith's shop, cottage and barn, and on the Heath a large fishpond called Ash Pool, a former sandpit.

Fig 5. The former carriage drive to Hindlip House

Fig 6. 16th Century Hindlip House

On the west side from Sandyway, the Bull Meadows, a barn, 'The Bull Inn', four open strips in the Widefield, Bents Close and ¾ acre of ground near Martin Brook.

'The Bull Inn' was probably a coaching inn situated in the garden of the present-day Fernhill Heath House with its bowling green on the opposite side of the road. Markets and fairs were held in both Worcester and Droitwich that brought passing trade to the Inn and the blacksmith.

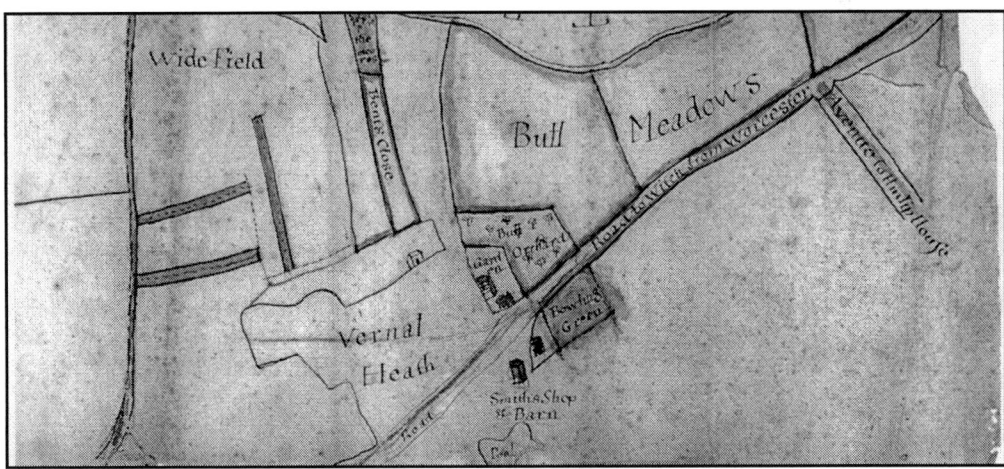

Fig 7. Sketch of 'The Bull Inn' and Bowling Green

Following the death of Thomas Morris, the licensee, in 1754, the Inn was taken over by William Surman. Repairs to the Inn were necessary and Joseph Priddey of Droitwich submitted his estimate, which also included building a new cart house, repairing the barn and stable. The estimate gives a picture of a building with cellars, pantry, parlour and rooms above, a thatched roof and chimneys. Repairs included raising the parlour chimney to 4 ft. Repairing the thatch on the north side of the house to cover two bays, and on the west side to cover one bay. Making a brick cistern to hold 3 hogsheads. Sinking a cellar where the pantry was, 9 feet x 7 feet x 2 feet 6 inches deep with a support to the cellar under the Summer (a beam running from wall to wall) and repairing the cellar floor. Making a door to the parlour and one to the passage. Repairing the quarry floor. Wanting in the Parlour chamber floorboards 12 x 4. Coiling the pantry floor between the joists 12 x 12. Repairing several walls, whitewashing several rooms, repairing the Inn sign and re-glazing the windows where necessary.

The size of the new cart house to be built was 21 feet x 14 feet and thatched. Repairing the barn with new plank flooring 18 feet x 12 feet, repairing two shutters and several walls, and the thatched roof on the west side. Repairing the walls of the stable and fitting one sill 10 feet long.

On the opposite side of the road between the bowling green and the large fishpond was the blacksmith's shop and cottage rented by Edward Harcourt. The cost of repairs was included in the same estimate for the Inn.

Taking off the roof of the blacksmith's shop 13 x 12, repairing the tiling and chimney and the shop door. Repairing several walls of the house and whitewashing the rooms, and re-glazing where necessary.

The estimate concluded with a proviso to complete the above in a workmanlike manner and to find all the materials except timber that would be found on the premises.

Cost of repairing 'The Bull Inn' £22.1.3d. (£2,667.79p in 2000).
The blacksmith's shop and house £3.11.9d.[1] (£429.26p in 2000).

It is not known when the Inn ceased trading. In 1757 the Worcestershire Quarter Sessions removed Edward Harcourt and his family from Vernal

---

[1] *WRO. BA 2636. 47674. 1-12.*

Heath back to his birthplace at Westwood, near Droitwich.[2] The blacksmith's shop was later demolished and another one built by the side of the Ash Pool. It closed in the 1870s and the Mission Room was built on this site in 1879.

On the east side of the Heath was Oakeys Farm (later O'Keys Farm), 8 acres held by Charles Reynolds.

On the west side, 28 acres called Chapmans & Swynesland (later The Cedars) were held by William Badeley of Common Hill House, Claines, his wife, Penelope, had inherited the farm in 1741 from her father, Joseph Weston of Worcester. An Abstract of Title dated 1753 described the farm as one messuage (house) and nook called Chapmans, 2 messuages and a nook called Swynesland.

To the southeast was The Hurst Ground (later Hurst Farm), 13½ acres, held by George Reynolds. The Hurst Ground took its name from a long narrow strip of woodland between the Hindlip/Claines boundary of the old Roman road and the cart track to the farm. An entry in the 1782 Claines and Whistones Manor Rental Books described the farm as 'A cottage and three closes, one Vernella [sic] – a narrow and straight way, and one parcel called the Hempbutts called the Hurst'.

Mr. Wylde held Spellis Farm, 97 acres of freehold and copyhold. Spellis is a corruption of the name 'Spellye'. A Richard Spellye of Claines received a grant of land in 1302 for service as Bailiff of Whistone tithing.

The Widefield and Perry-field

On the west side of Vernal Heath was the Widefield that spread over a wide area from the end of the present-day Post Office Lane to the lower half of Links Lane to the parish boundary with Martin Hussingtree and westwards towards Lower Town. A track from (Post Office Lane) through the Widefield joined up with the track to Lower Town. Kennels Lane off Station Road, was formerly an open strip in the Widefield and opened up as a lane in 1868 for access to the newly built Worcestershire Hunt Kennels and joined the track to Lower Town. There were numerous other strips in several ownerships in Perry-field, now Perrycroft Close, Broadfield Crescent and Shrawley Road area. These open fields were apportioned into numerous narrow strips of land and held by copyholders through an ancient Anglo Saxon tenure. The strips passed yearly to a

---

[2] WRO. Quarter Sessions. 1757.

fresh owner so that each in turn should hold every strip for one season's crops and none should have an unfair preference in the quality of the soil.

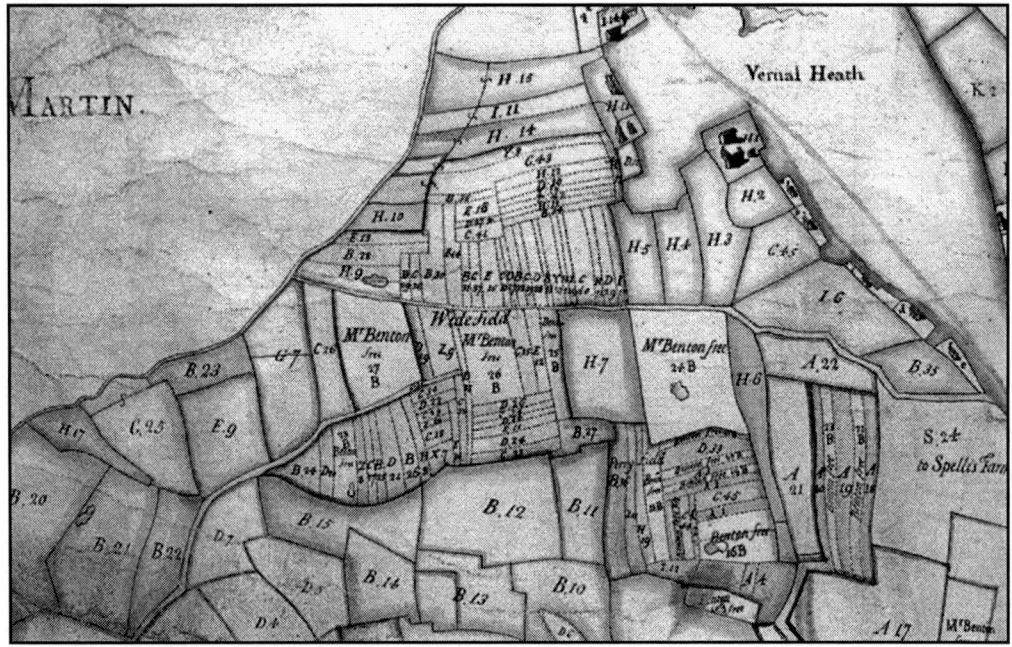

Fig 8. Widefield and Perry-field open strips

On the east side of Red Hill The Revd. Dekyn held 8 acres of copyhold land.

On the north side of the present-day Dilmore Lane John Jew occupied a copyhold cottage on 1 rood of land. Between Dilmore Lane and Red Hill were two enclosed fields, the Dillmoor and Great Dillmoor, a Saxon name referring to the moorland and the dill herb that once grew there. The name 'Dilmore' was later to come into general usage for this particular area of Vernal Heath. West of John Jew's cottage were two enclosed fields, Sugar or Seg Close, once cold and sour land, and Deans Green (Danes Green), below which was a small open space, the last remaining area of the waste or common land of Deans Green.

The remainder of the enclosed copyhold and freehold land on the west side of Vernal Heath and Red Hill was in the possession of several owners and their tenants, viz.

Deans Green Farm owned by John Benton of Pebworth, Worcestershire. His wife, Mary*, had inherited this freehold farm from her mother, Mary

Walker nee Norton of Tutnall. Part of an inscription on a wall tablet in the chancel of St. Peter's Church, Pebworth, dedicated to the Eden family, relates that Mary Anne Millard Eden was the granddaughter of John Benton** who, through his mother, Mary, represented the Norton's of Claines. (This John Benton** was the grandson of Mary*).

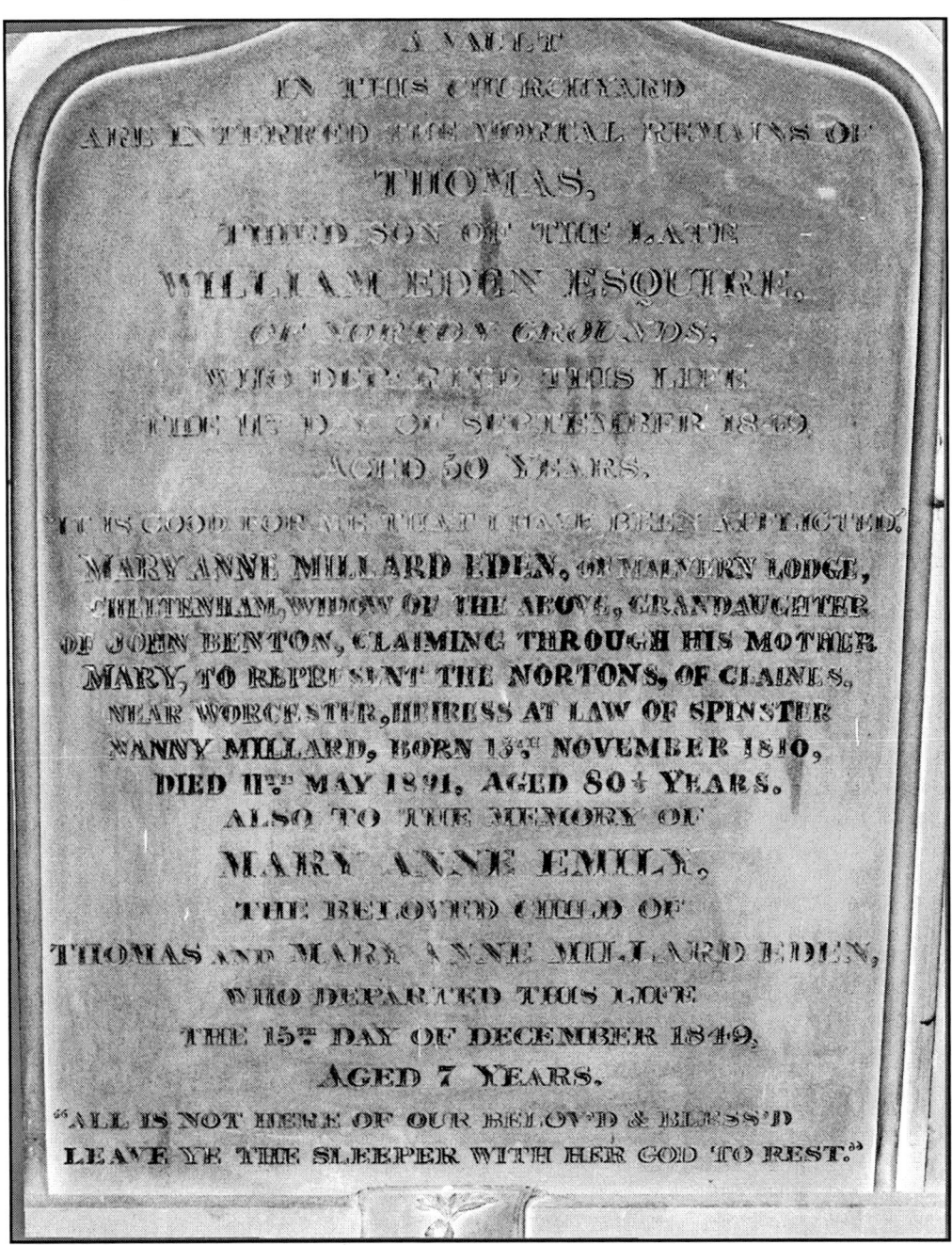

Fig 9. Wall Tablet in Pebworth church

John Benton owned 85 acres of freehold, and held several copyhold strips in the open fields of the Widefield and Perry Croft. In 1755 the farm, by then 100 acres, with a reduced rental from £52 to £46 per annum and occupied by John Gould was sold.

Thomas Vernon of Hanbury had purchased the manor of Shrawley, Worcestershire, in 1700. In a codicil to his will dated 1720 he devised that £1,000 should be set apart for the benefit of the poor in the parishes of Hanbury and Shrawley for buying gowns, coal and other fuels for poor old men and women in the winter. The share in the parish of Shrawley was laid out in the purchase of Deans Green Farm. The Claines Tithe Map of 1840 records the farm as Danes Green and it is known by this name today.

The Charity Commissioners allowed the Shrawley Charity to sell the farm in 1918. Several properties in Station Road were built in the 1930s, the Shrawley Road estate off Station Road in the 1960s, and the Danes Green estate in the late 1990s/2000.

Mr. Robert Harrison of Bromsgrove held four farms –
1. Upper Tapenhall 68 acres of copyhold.
2. 56 acres of freehold known then as Puckpit Farm, later called Pulpit and afterwards The Grange (RGS).
3. Copyhold, acreage unknown and forming part of Puckpit. Charles Reynolds, Tenant.
4. Copyhold, acreage unknown, and forming part of Puck Pit.

Building lapsed during The Seven Years War (1756-63) against France, Russia, Austria and Saxony that ended in victory for England.

Building commenced again in 1763 but only on a very small scale with, probably, just two or three copyhold cottages built in a single year, the annual rent was increased to 2s 0d, although rents on properties built towards the end of the century, when the country was again at war with France, were reduced to 1s.0d payable to the Bishop of Worcester. The Manorial Courts at that time resisted all attempts to enclose the Heath and cottages were built on the waste, i.e. strips of land between the highway and the enclosed fields, on the Wich Road in Vernal Heath, on Red Hill and in Dilmore Lane. Anyone who wanted to build a cottage needed permission from the Court Baron. A letter of request signed by several landowners vouching that the intended cottager was a good, honest and hardworking person was presented to the Court for their consideration.

In 1797 John Partridge built a copyhold blacksmith's shop and house on a piece of land 63 yards long x 14 yards at its north end, and 4 yards broad at its south end on the waste on Red Hill (between the present-day Morton House and Dilmore House Hotel), with the rent reduced to 1s.0d per year. This was an ideal spot for a blacksmith's shop with the number of stagecoaches, carts and wains coming up or attempting descent of Red Hill. The following year John Partridge tried to enclose another piece of the waste as a garden but was ordered by the Manorial Court, along with other tenants, to take down the palings and return the land to its existing state. Encroachment upon the common waste without permission was an offence.

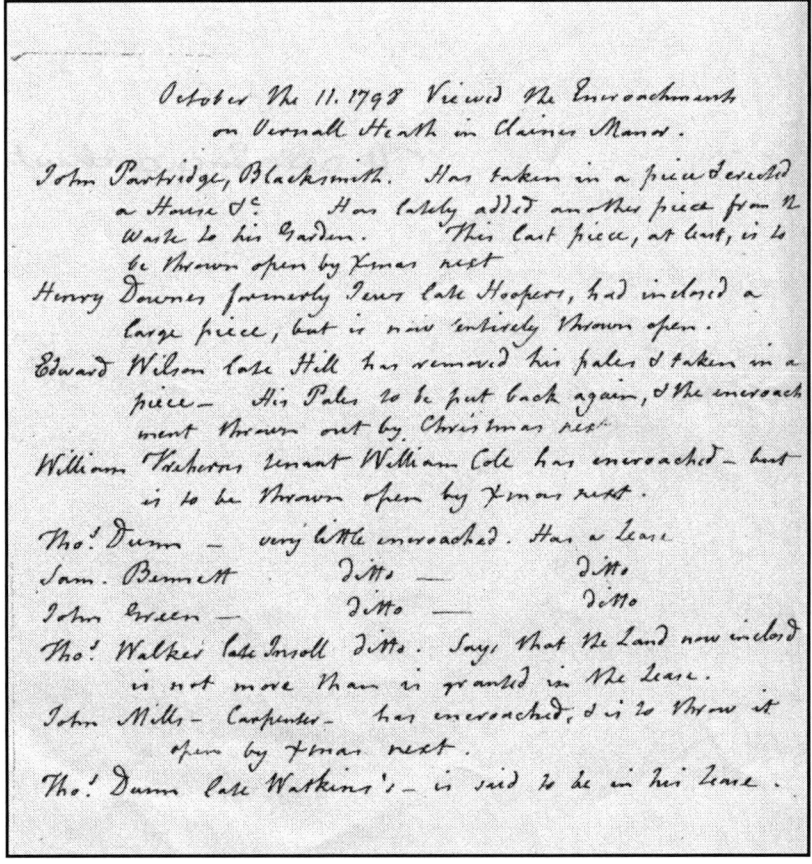

Fig 10. Encroachments 1798

The Hindlip Estate

Sir William Compton of Hindlip House died in 1758 and eventually his youngest daughter, Jane, inherited the Hindlip Estate. She married John Berkeley of Spetchley. Jane died in 1778 and John in 1780. Their two daughters, Catherine and Jane, leased Hindlip House in 1784 to a Mrs. Martin as a girls' boarding school for several years. Catherine died and Jane inherited the estate and married Lord Southwell in 1799.

Around 1818 Hindlip House was pulled down and a new Hindlip House was built further away from the old site. In 1828 the carriage drive to Hindlip House a little way south from Sandyway was stopped up[3] and nearer to Fearnall Heath a new carriage drive was opened and the gate-lodge built and occupied by a coachman and his wife who was responsible for opening and shutting the gates.

It was either John Berkeley or Lord Southwell who built Fearnall Heath House on the northern edge of the village. By 1803 the property was leased out as a school for young gentlemen.

> T. Weston respectfully informs his friends that he has taken FEARNAL HEATH HOUSE for the education of YOUNG GENTLEMEN where the Strictest Attention will be paid to their Health, Morals and Comfort, and every Execution used to promote their Advancement in Classical and Commercial knowledge. THE SCHOOL will be opened 24th inst, FEARNAL HEATH, Jan 6th 1803.
>
> *Worcester Herald. 6th January 1803.*

Perhaps it was to help to defray part of the costs of building his new Hindlip House that in 1825 Lord Southwell sold the Bull Meadows, Fearnall Heath House, a cottage near to the House, four cottages built on the former bowling green, together with Otter Hurst coppice, a small lake, and a cottage on the east side of Sandyway close to the parish boundary. James Williams an army surgeon and the brother of The Revd George Williams of Martin Hussingtree purchased this estate. James Williams did not live at Fearnall Heath House and for several years he probably continued to lease it out as a private school.

---

[3] *WRO. Quarter Sessions. 1828. Vol. II. Fols. 419 & 420.*

Fig 11. The Lodge

Fig 12. Carriage Drive

Chapter 3
From a Settlement to a Village

The Parish workhouse opened on Vernal Heath in 1813. (See Chapter 6). The year 1819 was particularly bad with a great many people out of work, homeless and in great need, who refused to enter the workhouse and moved onto the Heath where they set up makeshift shelters but were not forced to take them down. Spasmodic development gathered momentum from 1820 when small copyhold cottages were built on the Heath effectively enclosing most of the area and paying the lord of the manor, the Bishop of Worcester, either 1s.0d or 2s.0d annual rental and to the Claines Overseers, a poor levy, towards the upkeep of the poor. Within 20 years the settlement became a self-supporting village.

The Tithe Commutation Act 1836 and the 1841 Census

The aim of this Act was to convert traditional tithe payments based on one tenth of the annual produce of land or labour into rent payments of money to the clergy. Maps were drawn up to show parish boundaries with a Tithe Apportionment documenting land ownership, occupiers, plot numbers, a description of the land, state of cultivation, acreage and the amount of rent-charge payable. Before the Dissolution of the Monasteries 1536-39 the great or rectorial tithes of Claines were in the hands of St. Wulstan's Hospital (The Commandery, Worcester), but Henry VIII gave them to Christ Church, Oxford, which he was building at that time. At the end of the 18th century the tithes were sold to the Wakeman family of Perdiswell for £2,000 who owned them at the time of the passing of this Act. The lesser tithes had, at one time, been in the hands of the White Ladies Nunnery. After the Dissolution the tithes passed through various hands and some went to the Wylde family at The Commandery and to the Rector of St. Swithin's Church, Worcester. The tithes of Smite Farm were appropriated to St. Oswald's Hospital in Whistone tithing.

Several of the earlier place and field names listed in the 1751-53 terrier of the manor of Claines had changed, either from misinterpreting the broad local dialect or simply became known by the name of the tenant who had occupied the land. Dilmore was now a designated area within Fearnall Heath, Puck Pit Farm was called Pulpit Farm, Deans Green became Danes Green, the open Widefield was written as Wheatfield, the

Fig 13. Claines Tithe Map. 1840
Plot No. 43 Lodge, plantation and carriage drive to Hindlip House;
No. 74 Blacksmith's Shop; No. 75 Fishpond; No. 81 Fearnall Heath House;
No. 109 House, lawn etc., later called The Cedars; No. 261 Old Workhouse; Nos. 262 – 264 O'Key's Farm.

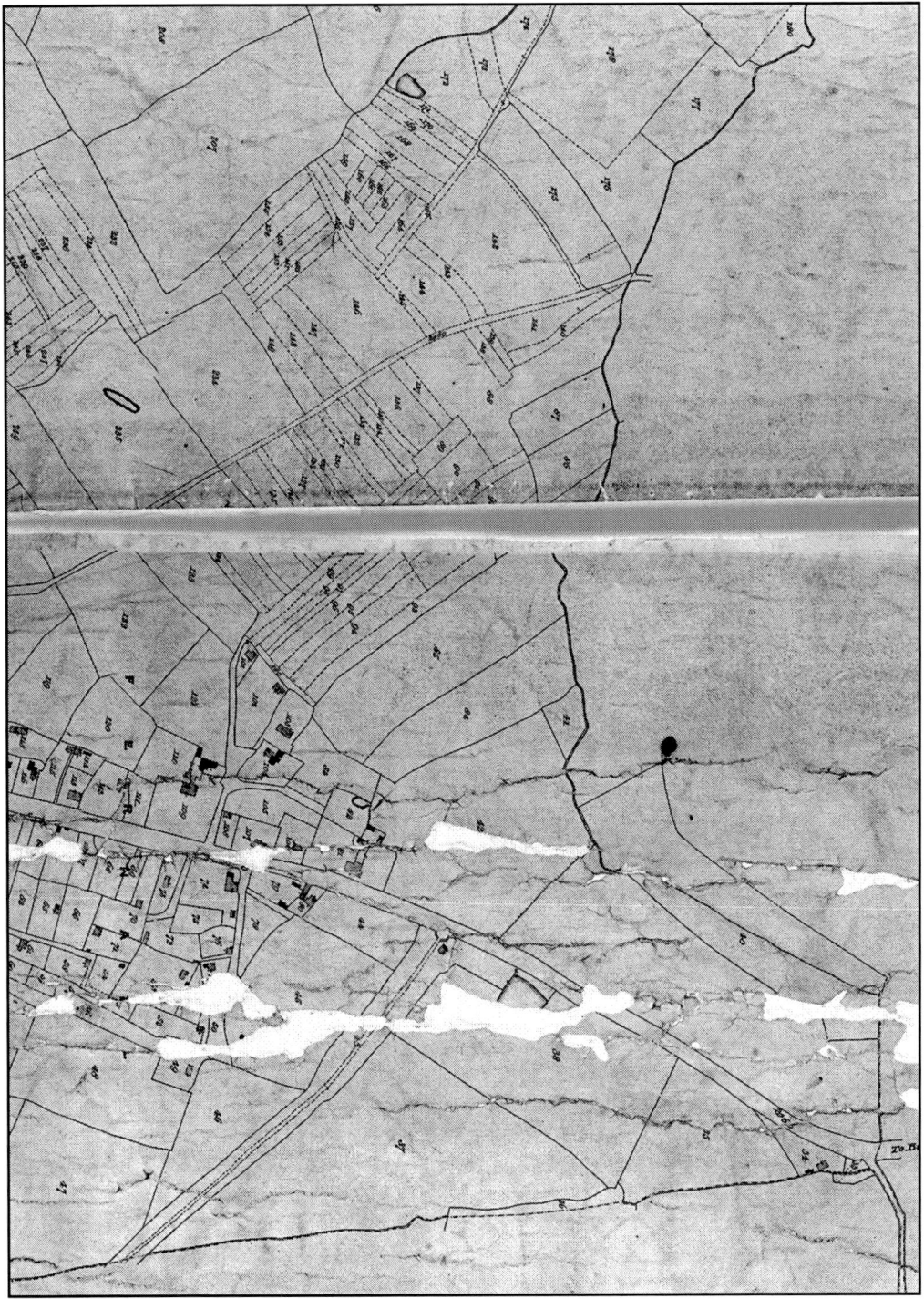

Fig 14. The Wheatfield formerly the Widefield
Plot Nos. 88 – 100 and 124 – 141   East side of Links Lane;
Nos. 14 – 174 West side of Links Lane.
Perry Field, Plot Nos. 229 – 233 and 237 – 248.

Wich-Way Close and Guit Stocking fields were now Copsons Land (on the Droitwich Road opposite Dilmore Lane), and Links Meadow was renamed Perry Croft.

Much of the layout of the village had taken shape with several cul-de-sacs off the Droitwich Road, later known as the present-day Post Office Lane. School Lane, then The Sling, and now Sling Lane. The track from The Sling to Hindlip was opened up later as a servants and tradesmen's entrance to Hindlip Hall. Chapel Lane – now O'Keys Lane; Live and Let Live Lane – now Ivy Lane; and The Butchers, later Butchers Lane and Butchers Opening – now Butchers Walk. All simple names and appropriate to each particular area.

The Heath was enclosed with about 90 dwellings built in the Post Office Lane area and along the front and behind on both sides of the Droitwich Road south from (Sling Lane) to the present railway bridge. A private school had opened and closed some years earlier near here. Some of the early cottages had been demolished and instead of being replaced with one, several smaller terraced dwellings were built on the same plot, other plots were divided up and built upon. For example, on the west side of the Heath shown on the 1751-53 map, a-e there were 5 cottages, by 1841 on 4 of the plots, a-d, there were 17 cottages, a house and a butcher's shop adjoining, all with gardens. On Plot e, the early cottage had been demolished and the plot was divided into two, one as a pig run and the other as a garden. The cottages were basic, either a living room and bedroom or a living room and kitchen with two bedrooms, and an earth closet outside. A shared washhouse and well. Some had a brewhouse and piggeries. The workhouse had closed and was occupied by a shoemaker with several apprentices. There were tailors and dressmakers, two general stores, two butchers' shops, two blacksmiths, one inn and three beerhouses.

Public Houses

The 'White Hart' is the oldest public house in the village. A cottage occupied this site in 1753 but there is no evidence that it was then an inn. The three beerhouses; one was the 'Plough Inn' which was near the old workhouse and later renamed the 'Live and Let Live', its name recalling the "Hungry 40s" and was the slogan for the Peel government used to repeal the Corn Laws of 1846. Another beerhouse was called the 'Hop

Pole that may have been the former school next door to the 'White Hart' and demolished when the railway was built, or one at Sandyway. The 1830 Beerhouse Act abolished tax on beer and anyone could apply for a license costing two guineas and turn their private house into a public house. The beerhouses were licensed to sell only on six days a week and were closed on Sundays. The beer was a sideline to the householders' main occupation and it was usually the wife who sold it. Later the licensees applied for full licences to sell beers, wines and spirits.

Red Hill and Dilmore

Development on Red Hill and Dilmore had not kept pace with the village area around the Heath and the old workhouse. On Red Hill, Oakfield House, a freehold mansion and grounds, was leased out to Mrs. Mary Marmont as a girls' boarding school called Oakfield Academy. There was the blacksmith's shop and house. In 1835 the Nonconformist church, Lady Huntingdon's Connexion of Birdport, Worcester, erected a chapel or a 'village station' costing £125 with free sittings for 100 people onto an 18th century cottage.[1] The Chapel closed in the 1850s and was turned into a cottage.

On the subject of chapels, another 'village station' attached to the Congregational Church in Angel Street, Worcester, opened at Fearnall Heath in 1860 but there is no record of where this chapel was situated or who were the leading figures; although documents recorded that in 1868 there were 52 children and 59 the following year in the Sunday school.[2]

1841 Census – Fearnall Heath	
Males under 10 years	27
Males over 10 years	95
Females under 10 years	44 including 3 boarders at Oakfield Academy
Females over 10 years	146 including 17 boarders at Oakfield Academy
Total number of residents	**312 including 20 boarders**

[1] 1851 Ecclesiastical Census.
[2] Angel Congregational – Worcester City United Reform Church. 'A Particular Church of Worcester'. Revd John M. March.

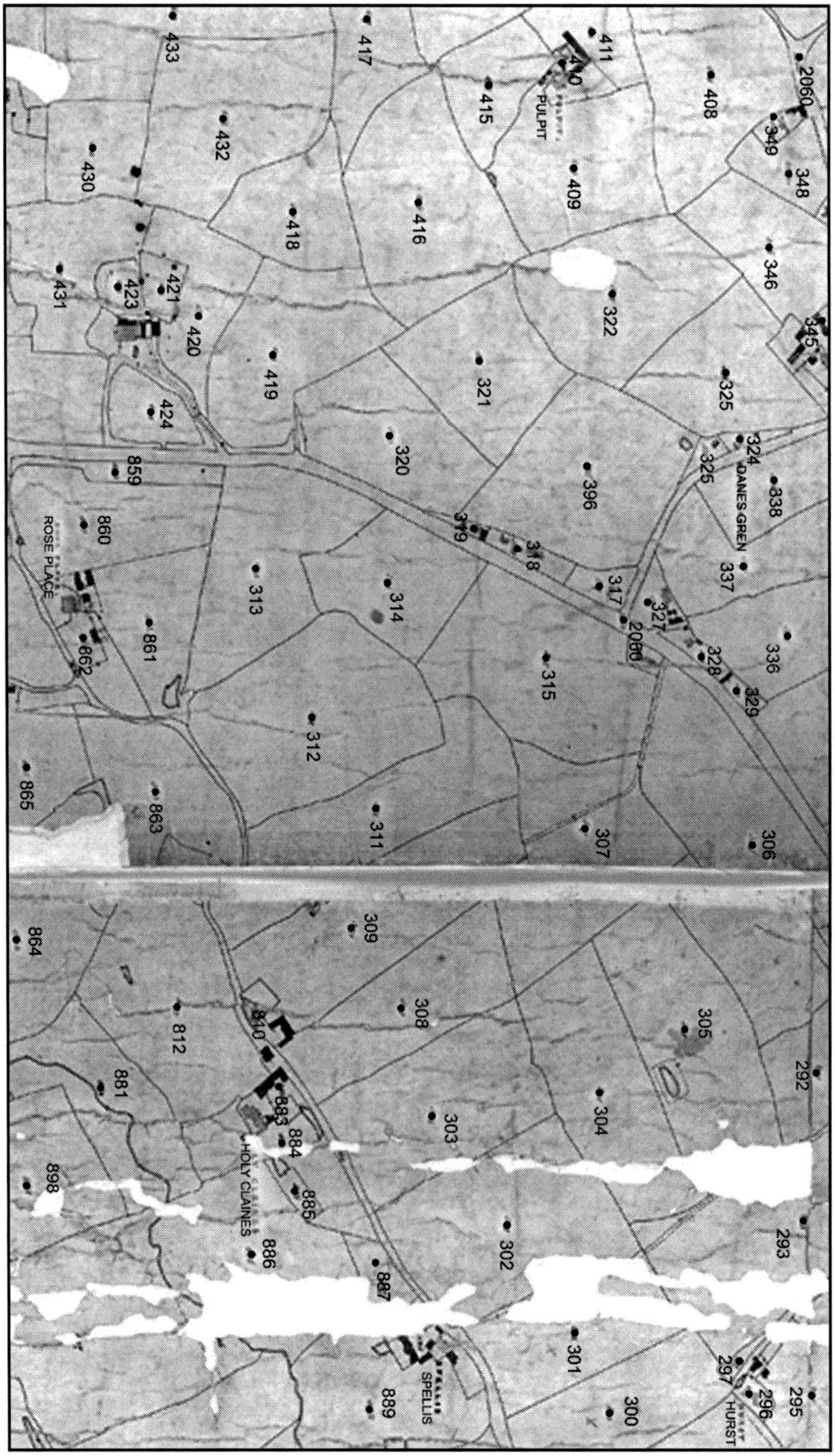
PULPIT
ROSE PLACE
DANES GREN
HOLY CLAINES
SPELLIS
HURST
433
417
411
410
415
408
2060
432
430
349
348
409
418
416
346
431
423
421
420
322
345
419
321
325
424
320
324
325
838
859
396
860
319
318
337
317
327
313
314
2060
336
861
328
862
315
329
312
865
863
311
307
306
864
309
812
308
305
292
881
810
883
304
303
884
898
885
293
886
302
887
301
297
296
295
889
300

At the junction of Dilmore Lane, both Laburnum Cottage and Dilmore Lodge (demolished in 1978) replaced two earlier cottages. Next to Dilmore Lodge was a beer and cider house called 'The Old House at Home' (now Pear Tree House), and then Tapenhall House.

Opposite Dilmore Lane and down the lane were several cottages built in an earlier age. Some of the cottages in Dilmore Lane were altered to take in another family. Nurses, village women, who helped out at the beginning and ending of life, occupied two of the cottages. The village pound for stray animals was situated opposite them. It was a condition of the manor that no animals were left unattended on the common land. Any stray animals were impounded and a fine paid to the lord of the manor before the animals were released back to their owners.

Fig 15 (opposite page). Claines Tithe Map 1840

Red Hill.
Plot No. 420 Homestead; No. 423 Oakfield Academy; No. 319 Blacksmith's Shop; No. 318 Cottage and Lady Huntingdon's Chapel; No. 317 Cottage and garden.

Dilmore Lane.
Dilmore.
Plot No. 327 Dilmore House, later called Dilmore Lodge, Thorneycroft and Heddon House; No. 328 'The Old House at Home' later Pear Tree House; No. 329 Tapenhall House.
Opposite Dilmore Lane, Plot No. 316, 3 cottages and gardens.

The Oxford, Worcester and Wolverhampton Railway

The idea of a railway line from Oxford, via Worcester to Wolverhampton was first mooted in 1844 and an Act of Parliament was passed in 1845 to build the line. From the beginning the line was beset with financial problems and which gauge to use, either Stephenson's standard gauge of 4'8½" or Brunel's broad gauge of 7'0", as it was apparent by then that a uniformity of gauge throughout the country was required. Isambard Kingdom Brunel, the chief engineer of the Great Western Railway, met shareholders at the Guildhall, Worcester, in May 1844, to persuade them to back his broad gauge. An Act of Parliament was passed to lay Brunel's gauge but it was Stephenson's gauge that was actually used.

Very few landowners were affected by the building of the railway line through Fearnall Heath in the late 1840s and were, of course, compensated for the loss of land and properties. Two cottages and the beerhouse on the east side of the Droitwich Road were demolished to make way for the new railway line and bridge, but the 'White Hart' was saved, it was owned by Edward Tandy who also sold provisions to the navvies working below on the new railway. Almost opposite a new beerhouse was built, the 'Durham Ox' to take advantage of the navvies too. It may have been the locals who nicknamed the 'Durham Ox' the 'Bull' and the name was later changed for that reason. The 'Half Way House' opened later.

The railway incline down to Worcester begins just north of the modern footbridge, and the superb workmanship of the navvies can easily be seen where they cut through the land to take the line forward. Many tons of soil were shifted and used to shore up embankments in the vicinity. The railway bridge supporting the main Worcester to Droitwich road was built to a very high standard that lasted well and it was not until 1978 that major repairs were necessary and again in 1994. The line north of the modern footbridge cut through the ancient Widefield or Wheatfield.

By 1852 only part of the railway had been completed, that between Stourbridge and Evesham, a total length of 36 miles, with 9 stations including these two towns and Fearnall Heath. On the 1st May 1852 a special train ran between Stourbridge and Evesham. All along the line many places were decorated with flags and flowers and at the stations there were groups of people cheering the train, but it was Evesham that

Fig 16. Fernhill Heath Station

Fig 17. Fernhill Heath Station

led the celebrations with two great feasts laid on for this important occasion.[3]

The main freight traffic handled by the railway at Worcester was coal, and Alexander Clunes Sheriff, Manager of the Oxford, Worcester and Wolverhampton Railway Company with others set up the South Wales & Cannock Chase Coal Company in 1861 and established an agency at Fearnall Heath Station, building a railway siding for this purpose.

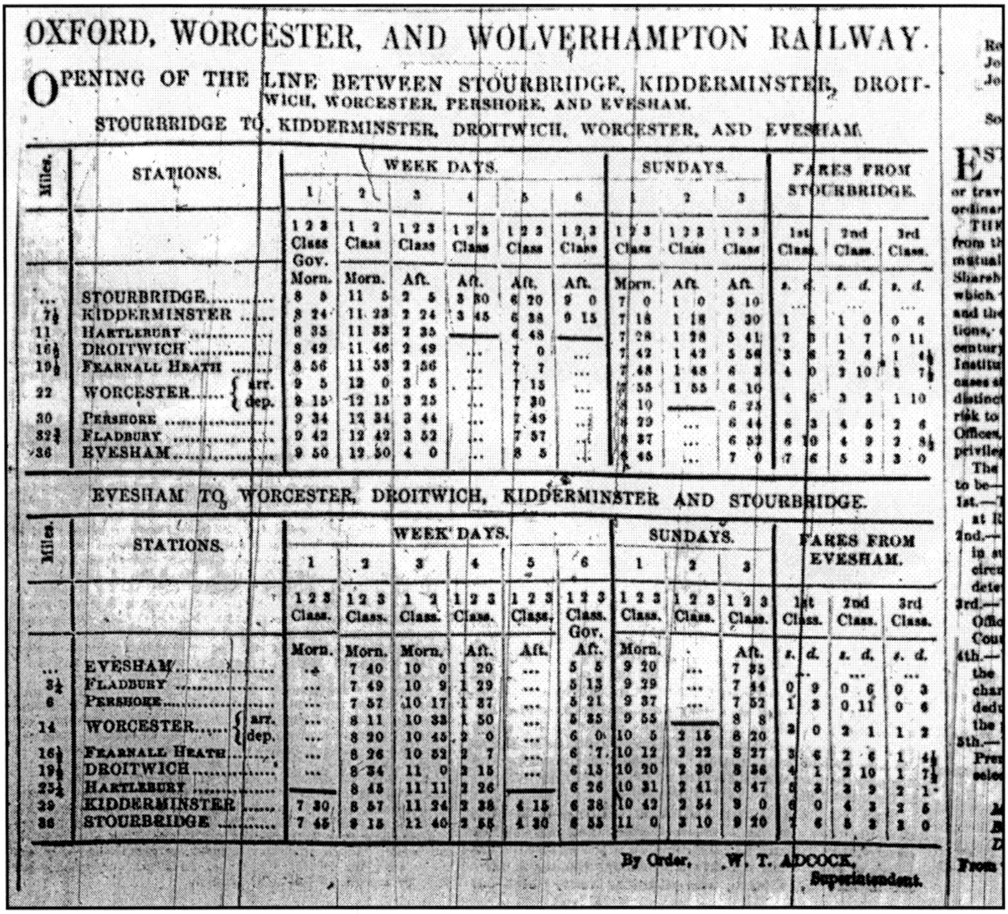

OXFORD, WORCESTER, AND WOLVERHAMPTON RAILWAY.

OPENING OF THE LINE BETWEEN STOURBRIDGE, KIDDERMINSTER, DROITWICH, WORCESTER, PERSHORE, AND EVESHAM.

STOURBRIDGE TO KIDDERMINSTER, DROITWICH, WORCESTER, AND EVESHAM.

Miles.	STATIONS.	Week Days 1	2	3	4	5	6	Sundays 1	2	3	Fares from Stourbridge 1st Class	2nd Class	3rd Class
		1 2 3 Class Gov.	1 2 Class	1 2 3 Class	1 2 3 Class	1 2 3 Class	1 2 3 Class	1 2 3 Class	1 2 3 Class	1 2 3 Class			
		Morn.	Morn.	Aft.	Aft.	Aft.	Aft.	Morn.	Aft.	Aft.	s. d.	s. d.	s. d.
...	STOURBRIDGE	8 5	11 5	2 5	3 30	6 20	9 0	7 0	1 0	5 10	...	...	...
7½	KIDDERMINSTER	8 24	11 23	2 24	3 45	6 38	9 15	7 18	1 18	5 30	1 6	1 0	0 6
11	HARTLEBURY	8 35	11 33	2 35	——	6 48	——	7 28	1 28	5 41	2 3	1 7	0 11
16½	DROITWICH	8 49	11 46	2 49	...	7 0	...	7 42	1 42	5 56	3 6	2 4	1 4½
19½	FEARNALL HEATH	8 56	11 53	2 56	...	7 7	...	7 48	1 48	6 3	4 0	2 10	1 7½
22	WORCESTER arr.	9 5	12 0	3 5	...	7 15	...	7 55	1 55	6 10	4 6	3 3	1 10
	WORCESTER dep.	9 15	12 15	3 25	...	7 30	...	8 10	——	6 25			
30	PERSHORE	9 34	12 34	3 44	...	7 49	...	8 29	...	6 44	6 3	4 5	2 6
32¾	FLADBURY	9 42	12 42	3 52	...	7 57	...	8 37	...	6 53	6 10	4 9	2 8½
36	EVESHAM	9 50	12 50	4 0	...	8 5	...	8 45	...	7 0	7 6	5 3	3 0

EVESHAM TO WORCESTER, DROITWICH, KIDDERMINSTER AND STOURBRIDGE.

Miles.	STATIONS.	Week Days 1	2	3	4	5	6	Sundays 1	2	3	Fares from Evesham 1st Class	2nd Class	3rd Class
		1 2 3 Class.	1 2 3 Class.	1 2 Class.	1 2 3 Class.	1 2 3 Class.	1 2 3 Class. Gov.	1 2 3 Class.	1 2 3 Class.	1 2 3 Class.			
		Morn.	Morn.	Morn.	Aft.	Aft.	Aft.	Morn.		Aft.	s. d.	s. d.	s. d.
...	EVESHAM	...	7 40	10 0	1 20	...	5 5	9 20	...	7 35	...	...	...
3½	FLADBURY	...	7 49	10 9	1 29	...	5 13	9 29	...	7 44	0 9	0 6	0 3
6	PERSHORE	...	7 57	10 17	1 37	...	5 21	9 37	...	7 52	1 3	0 11	0 6
14	WORCESTER arr.	...	8 11	10 33	1 50	...	5 35	9 55	——	8 8	2 0	2 1	1 2
	WORCESTER dep.	...	8 20	10 45	2 0	...	6 0	10 5	2 15	8 20			
16½	FEARNALL HEATH	...	8 26	10 52	2 7	...	6 7	10 12	2 23	8 27	3 6	2 6	1 4½
19½	DROITWICH	...	8 34	11 0	2 15	...	6 15	10 20	2 30	8 36	4 1	2 10	1 7½
23½	HARTLEBURY	——	8 45	11 11	2 26	——	6 26	10 31	2 41	8 47	5 3	3 9	2 1
29	KIDDERMINSTER	7 30	8 57	11 24	2 38	4 15	6 38	10 42	2 54	9 0	6 0	4 3	2 6
36	STOURBRIDGE	7 45	9 15	11 40	2 55	4 30	6 55	11 0	3 10	9 20	7 6	5 3	3 0

By Order, W. T. ADCOCK, Superintendent.

Fig 18. 1854 Railway Timetable

The railway brought much needed prosperity to the village at a time when there was agricultural distress, although very few houses were built during this period. The earliest railway employees came from outside Fearnall Heath and the county and some settled here. The railway company only ever provided three tied houses for its employees in the

---

[3] *Worcester Herald. 2nd May 1852.*

village; a pair of semi-detached cottages in O'Keys Lane and a cottage (now demolished) built on the southeast railway embankment next to the railway bridge, other railway employees found rented accommodation elsewhere in the village.

The trains stopped regularly at Fearnall Heath providing a good service and effectively turned it into a 19th century 'commuter village'. When Fearnall Heath House was put up for sale in 1853 the advertisement included 'Close to a Railway Station'.

Wake Sundays

Up until the late 1850s there was an annual tradition of celebrating Wake Sunday held on Trinity Sunday at Claines Church. The Wakes were held in the churchyard and money was generally allowed from the church accounts to celebrate this event that usually managed to get completely out of hand with scenes of fighting, drunkenness and debauchery. In 1750 the principal inhabitants assembled in the Vestry and agreed to forfeit 40 shillings each if they did not use 'their utmost endeavour to put a stop to the evil practices commonly committed on our Wake Sunday.' The public stocks were used for the last time in 1853 when a cowman from Spellis Farm occupied them for being outrageously drunk at the Wake. After that all that remained of the Wakes was a little dancing carried on in Fearnall Heath and that gradually faded out.[4]

The Fearnall Heath District Farmers' Society

In an attempt to educate agricultural labourers this Society was founded in 1847. The Society arranged annual competitions in all aspects of farm work; ploughing, drilling, mowing, reaping, rick building, thatching, hedging and ditching etc on local farms. Long service awards were given to both male and female workers, and for attendance at church. Members dined together at the 'White Hart', the 'Hadley Bowling Green' or at a farm to discuss topical agricultural subjects. The Society disbanded about 1859.[5]

---

[4] *Notes and Queries for Worcestershire.* John Noake. 1856.
[5] *The History of Worcestershire Agriculture and Rural Evolution.*   R. C. Gaut. 1939.

The Hindlip Estate

In 1860 Lord Southwell of Hindlip House died, his wife Jane, having predeceased him in 1853. Soon after his death a public auction was held to sell off the livestock and farming implements. The House was leased out and later sold to Henry Allsopp, a brewer from Derbyshire who, for health reasons, had moved into Worcestershire to take the waters at Malvern.

On moving to Hindlip House he changed the name of the property to Hindlip Hall. Henry Allsopp expanded the Hindlip Estate into the village on the east side by buying up land and property whenever it came onto the market. He also purchased the Fearnall Heath House estate including the cottage and land at Sandyway. He brought the enlarged Hindlip Estate up to date by extensively building new houses and improving cottages and farm buildings. His workers' houses in particular were said to be amongst the best in the county and can still be seen today in the village near Hindlip School and in the parishes of Hindlip and Martin Hussingtree. The houses are particularly attractive with their distinctive eaves and the stone plaque of Henry Allsopp's monogram on some of the house walls.

The pair of semi-detached houses in Hurst Lane was built later in 1901.

The Worcestershire Hunt Kennels together with stables, a huntsman's house and cottages were built off Links Lane in 1866-68 by subscription. In 1868 Henry Allsopp became Joint Master of the Hunt with Sir Harry Vernon of Hanbury Hall but retired on account of poor health during the 1872-73 season. In 1869 he built a school at Sandyway for his estate workers' children, and in 1879 a Mission Room was erected in the village with 200 sittings at a cost to himself of £1,200.

The early 1870s brought another slump in farming that was to last until World War I and Henry Allsopp, in common with many landowners, reduced his tenants' rents.

In 1880 Queen Victoria conferred upon Henry Allsopp a baronetcy in recognition of his service to his country and as late Conservative MP for East Worcestershire. To celebrate this event the residents decorated the village with arches with messages of congratulation, flags and bunting. He was to have arrived at Shrub Hill, Worcester, railway station on the 21st April at 6 o'clock in the evening but was delayed and did not return until 10 o'clock. The effect to which the decorations were intended was lost but the enthusiasm of the villagers was not lessened and a large crowd

Fig 19. Henry Allsopp's houses. 1956.

waited to greet the new baronet on Fernhill Heath railway bridge. Upon his arrival the horses were taken from the shafts and men drew his carriage to the Hall. At the lodge gates a congratulatory address was read out which he acknowledged, and then moved on to the Hall where he thanked his tenants for the hearty greeting they had given him.[6] A peerage was conferred upon him in 1886 and he took the title Lord Hindlip.

On the 3rd April 1887 Lord Hindlip died. It had been intended that his funeral should be private at Hindlip Church but a large number of friends, members of the Worcestershire Hunt, Worcester citizens, tenants and villagers, representatives of his staff from Burton-upon-Trent, and others attended.[7]

The Hon. Samuel Charles Allsopp, MP, succeeded Lord Hindlip. The Hindlip family retained an interest in the village until the death of Agatha, Lady Hindlip in 1962.

---

[6] *Worcester Herald. 24th April 1860.*
[7] *Worcester Herald. 5th April 1887.*

The Fearnall Heath Brickyard in Hurst Lane owned by E. P. Webb of Evesham produced large quantities of tiles and drainpipes for land drainage and the 2nd Lord Hindlip later purchased the business. By the end of the 19th century the 3rd Lord Hindlip was the largest landowner in the area. The Hindlip Estate comprised of farms in Hindlip. O'Keys and The Hurst Farms, several cottages, Fernhill Heath House and the brickyard in Fernhill Heath. Spellis Farm in Claines. Martin Hall and Hill House Farms, and several cottages in Martin Hussingtree. Blackpole Farm near Worcester. Two public houses, the 'White Hart' at Fernhill Heath and the 'Pear Tree' at Smite.[8]

Building land

The large Perdiswell Estate, near Worcester, owned by Sir Offley Wakeman, was sold by auction in 1876. Included in the sale were five building plots in Fernhill Heath next to the railway cottage and fronting the Droitwich Road together with 20 acres of land on Red Hill opposite and next to Morton House, a mansion built in 1853-4 and the home of Thomas Barnaby.[9] The five pieces of building land were sold for £300, £315, £310, £260 and £280 and the 20 acres for £1,850, to him. Later only two of the plots were built on, those next to the railway cottage, the properties were called Highfield House and Stoneycroft Cottage. The remaining plots were gradually developed from 1908 to the 1930s.

The first house to be built in Links Lane (Station Lane then Station Road) was Firlands Lodge in the 1870s. The open strips in the Wheatfield (Widefield) were gradually sold off, and one property built in 1898, No. 52, Wheatfield Villa, was aptly named. A new style of housing had come into vogue, the villa, and several more detached and semi-detached villas were built in Links Lane and along the Droitwich Road.

North Claines Parish Council

In 1885 the City of Worcester was extended northwards into Claines with its new boundary at Astwood, Bilford Road, Droitwich Road, Checketts Lane, Ombersley Road and part of Northwick to the River Severn. Land south of the boundary went into Worcester and north of the boundary became the county part or North Claines, a very rural area.

---

[8] *WRO. BA 9875/11.*
[9] *WRO. BA 2309/41 & 45.*

On the 4th December 1894 the inaugural meeting of the civil parish of North Claines was held, 30 nominees put forward their names and 13 were elected onto North Claines Parish Council. Joseph White, Elijah Tolley and William Powell represented Fernhill Heath.

The freeholders of North Claines had, by an ancient right, grazed their stock on Pitchcroft, Worcester. In 1897 the Parish Council sold the common rights to the City of Worcester. A condition of the sale was that the money raised should be used in some manner for the public benefit of the parish.

The Diamond Jubilee of Queen Victoria was celebrated in the same year and the Parish Council put forward three proposals to commemorate the occasion. To restore and re-hang the bells in Claines Church, purchase a field for a recreation ground or give a dinner to all those who were alive on the Queen's accession on the 20th June 1837. The proposal to restore and re-hang the bells was withdrawn and the recreation ground proposal was defeated. A dinner was given for the elderly, and a tea and a celebration mug given to school and Sunday school children on the 22nd June. An oak tree was planted in Claines churchyard.

In April 1900 the Parish Council paid £382 for just over 4 acres of land in Cornmeadow Lane, Claines, for a new recreation ground for the benefit of the residents of North Claines.[10]

---

[10] *WRO. BA 10533/1,2.*

Chapter 4
1900-1950

By 1901 there were 179 properties with the majority of housing in the village area. It had taken 60 years for Fernhill Heath to nearly double in size. There were 521 residents.

1841 and 1901 census		
	1841	**1901**
Males under 10 years	27	32
Males over 10 years	95	167
Females under 10 years	44	62
Females over 10 years	146	260
Total number of residents	312*	521
*Total includes 17 boarders at Oakfield Academy		

The village, although small, was a desirable place in which to live with newly built properties, a railway station, a police station, several shops, a bakery, post office, a blacksmith and four public houses. Villagers enjoyed a social life with its own cricket club that later amalgamated with Claines cricket club, and the Ombersley, Fernhill Heath and District Agricultural Society held shows at Ombersley. Concerts took place in Hindlip School and in the new Baptist Chapel.

The Baptist Chapel

On the 3rd September 1903 Mrs. Larkworthy laid the foundation stone for the Baptist Chapel in O'Keys Lane. Her brother, Captain Alexander Locke, had purchased the piece of land in 1895 and put it in trust for the purpose of some day erecting a Baptist Chapel upon it, but did not live to see the foundation stone laid. As far back as 1885 a group of people sympathetic to the Baptist movement began holding meetings in some of the cottages in the village. The chapel was completed in two months and opened on the 10th December 1903. A Brotherhood and Sisterhood started a Sunday school. Through the efforts of the Brotherhood a vestry was added in October 1913.[1]

---

[1] *History of the Baptist Church, Worcester. E. Berry, JP. 1914.*

Fig 20. Foundation stone, Baptist Chapel.

Fig 21. Baptist Chapel Concert 1914.

Figs 22 & 23. Road widening on Red Hill. 1913.

Droitwich Road

In 1905 The Worcester Tramways began operating an omnibus service from Worcester to Fernhill Heath during the summer months only.

With the increase in traffic major road widening works were carried out on the Droitwich Road in 1913. The following year the Birmingham and Midland Motor Omnibus Co. Ltd., (later the Midland 'Red') began a regular route through the village to Worcester and Droitwich.

World War I

War was declared on the 4th August 1914. In nearby Blackpole, Cadbury Brothers of Bournville, Birmingham, had some years earlier built a warehouse on the side of the canal that was requisitioned as a munitions factory making war weapons and many residents were employed there. Older pupils left Hindlip School to work on the local farms and Austrian prisoners of war were drafted in to help during 1915. Agricultural wages in 1914 were 16s.9d per week and by 1919 had risen to 36s.6d. In 1915 the Worcestershire War Agricultural Committee set up a food production scheme with a 'Ploughing Up' Campaign and agriculture enjoyed an upturn when the Government guaranteed prices for crops and introduced subsidies to boost farm output but these were withdrawn in 1921. Conscription began in 1916. The Summer Time Act was brought in the same year. In 1917 rationing began. The Women's Land Army was billeted at Court Farm, Hindlip.

Fernhill Heath War Memorial Hall

In March 1919 a village committee was set up to provide a lasting memorial to all those who had served and to those who gave their lives in the Great War. At the first public meeting it was resolved that a memorial should be built to benefit the young men with a later resolution added that they should also cater for girls and women. The committee registered themselves as a friendly society and another resolution was passed that the memorial should cater for the working people in the district. In 1920 a site was purchased for £200 but later the committee felt that it was too much for their purse and sold it for the price they had given for it. The purchaser later sold the land at a profit and handed this over to the fund. The site on which the Memorial Hall stands was purchased from the 3rd Lord Hindlip for £100 who had earlier given them £100. Money was raised through donations, fetes, social activities, and a 'buy a brick' scheme, and in three and a half years the Committee had raised £1,300. The main hall is entered through a porch and vestibule. Cloakrooms, toilets and a kitchen were built. There was then a permanent screen with an operating platform for cinema shows. H. Percy Smith of Foregate Street, Worcester, was the architect, and Spicers of Droitwich Road, Worcester, built the hall. The final cost of the hall including furniture and fittings was about £2,300.

On Thursday, 28th September 1922, Sergt George Wyatt, VC, late of the 3rd Coldstream Guards, opened The Fernhill Heath and District Memorial Hall at which all the villagers seemed to have assembled outside. The ceremony commenced with a short service conducted by the Rector of Martin Hussingtree, The Revd F. O. Gascoigne.

The key of the hall was handed to Sergt Wyatt who declared the hall open "In commemoration of those men who had fought for their country in its time of peril." He concluded by saying, "I hope that no one will ever enter these doorways without giving a thought to the men who had made such a supreme sacrifice."[2]

The village and the surrounding parishes of Hindlip and Martin Hussingtree had rallied to the war effort with 154 men serving their country, of whom, 24 were killed, and all their names are commemorated on the Roll of Honour in Fernhill Heath War Memorial Hall.

The names of several of the men who lost their lives are also recorded on the Rolls of Honour in Hindlip School, Hindlip and Martin Hussingtree churches and the large war memorial erected in Claines churchyard.

There were no financial benefits handed out to the men who returned home from the war but Mrs. Dorothy Wilde, wife of the licensee of the 'Half Way House', on behalf of the British Legion, did a great deal of welfare work for the ex-servicemen of the village.

---

[2] *Worcester Evening News & Times. 28th September 1922.*

Fig 24. Roll of Honour, Fernhill Heath War Memorial
The left hand Memorial depicts 'Peace'

FERNHILL HEATH WAR MEMORIAL
Memoria in eternal

Boughton, R.	Clarke, G.	Edgecombe H.	Kettley, H.
Bruton, W.	Clinton, T.	Harper, B.	Russell, J.
Burrows, A.	Conn, C.	Hartland, M.	Lane, P.

Army

Barton, G.	Cummings, C.	Hindlip Charles Baron	
Barton, W.	Davis H.	Hartland, W.	Kettle, H.
Barton, Ar.	Davis, W.	Higgins, T.	Lamb, D.
Barton, A.	Dobern, A.	Hooper, G.	Lamb, W.
Barton, Alf.	Dobern, J.	Hope, W.	Lane, Hor.
Batchelor, J.	Dobern, H.	Hudson, G.	Lane, W.
Bridge, W.	Farley, H.	Insall, G.	Lane, H.
Brazier, P.	Gould, W.	Insall, W.	Lane, S.
Brown, A.	Griffiths, A.	Jones, A.	Lane, T.
Burrows, G.	Gunnell, E.	Jones, B.	Langley, J.
Cartridge, A.	Hanson, G.	Jones, W.	Lee, R.
Clee H.	Hanson, W.	Jones, O.	Medway, G.
Clifford, J.	Harris, A.	Keatley, T.	Millington, W
Clinton H.	Harper, A	Keatley, Hn.	Munslow. J.
Crumpton F.	Hartland, A	Keatley, Bert.	Munslow, T.
Carr, W.A.	Carpenter, L.	Keatley, H.	Newman, W
		Lamb, E.	

Erected in memory of the men of Fernhill Heath and District who fell in the Great War and in memory of those who served their Country in that time of peril and by the will of God returned safely home.

Fig 25. Roll of Honour, Fernhill Heath War Memorial
Right hand Memorial depicts 'St. George'

FERNHILL HEATH WAR MEMORIAL
Memoria in eternal

Lee, S.	Shepherd, G.	Vaughan, T.	Wheeler, R.
Mantle, B.	Stephens, T.	Vigors, P.	Williams, A.
Roberts, E.	Tranter, A.	Weston, T.	Woolley, E.

Army

Nind, A.	Rayner, D.	Tyler, S.	Wild, H.
Nind, H.	Sanderson, E.	Wale, H.	Wyatt, G. VC.
Noond, E.	Saunders, A.	Hope, P.	Wyatt, R. ??
Papworth, G.	Saunders, J.	Walker, G.	Wyatt, A.
Drake, W.K.	Saunders, W.	Walker, S.	Wynne, H.
Pitson, G.	Shepherd, H.	Walker, E.	Veales, H.
Powell, Hd.	Shepherd H.	Walker, R.	**Navy**
Powell, H.	Stanton, G.	Waters, H.	Griffiths, W.
Powell, H.J.	Stanton, G.	Weston, W.	Jones, E.
Reeves, R.R.	Stockton, H.	Weston, J.	Newey, D.
Reeves, A.	Smith, G.	Weston, P.	Newey, C.
Robson, W.	Smith, W.	Whalcott, W.	Prothero, E.
Rothnie, A.	Tarpler, W.	Wheeler, R.	Purdy, P.
Richards, F.	Teare, H.	Whittall, A.	Truby, H.
Richards, G.	Tho??ber-ugh, O.	Wilson, J.	Whatell, S.
Rushage, R.	Turner, G.	Wiggin, T.	Wilson, A.

Not of Gold, but only men can make a people great and strong and all who use this Hall ever remember the Noble Sacrifice and unselfish Devotion of the men to whose memory it is erected.

Fig 26. Mrs. Dorothy Wilde and friends of the Half Way Public House.

Danes Green Farm and The Grange (Formerly Puck Pit and Pulpit Farm)

Danes Green Farm was put up for sale in 1918 and auctioned off in 11 lots. Mrs. Emily Vigors of The Grange purchased Lot 1, Danes Green Farmhouse with outbuildings and just over 16 acres of land for £1,620. W. P. Cave of Tapenhall Farm and Caulin Court, Ladywood, purchased Lots 4, 5, 6, 7 and 9, amounting to approximately 38 acres of arable accommodation land and building sites for £1,815.

Mrs. Vigors died soon afterwards and The Grange Estate including Danes Green Farm was put on the market in August 1919. Bidding for The Grange reached £6,500 and Danes Green Farm £1,850, both were withdrawn because the offers were too low.

Col. Chichester privately purchased The Grange. After moving in he applied to the Archdiocese of Birmingham for a rescript to open a private Oratory in his new home. Permission was given in Rome at St. Peter's under the Seal of the Fisherman on the 20th December 1919. The Oratory was dedicated to Our Lady of Lourdes and St. Gerard Majella as a Chapel of Ease to Worcester St. George's Roman Catholic Church.[3] Visiting priests from Worcester, the Cotswolds and later the Sacred Heart, Droitwich, celebrated Mass with Col. Chichester's family, servants and local residents. Now elderly, one former resident remembers, as a child going to Mass, and afterwards was always taken into the kitchen by the maid and given a glass of milk before returning home. The chapel closed in 1981.[4]

New housing

After the war came the Depression with a slump in farming and a shortage of agricultural workers, with a great many farms sold off to pay death duties. The value of land fell. A piece of building land in Station Road sold for 5d (2p) per square yard in 1926.

Some cottages were little more than slums and a housing programme to clear them began and several sites were looked at on which to build new houses. A 1½-acre site in Dilmore Lane offered at 7d (3p) per square yard was not taken up.[5] Sites in Danes Green, the rear of Pear Tree House on

---

[3] *Archdiocese of Birmingham. Ref. P334/T9.*
[4] *Archdiocese of Birmingham Directory 1981.*
[5] *WRO. BA 6319/10.*

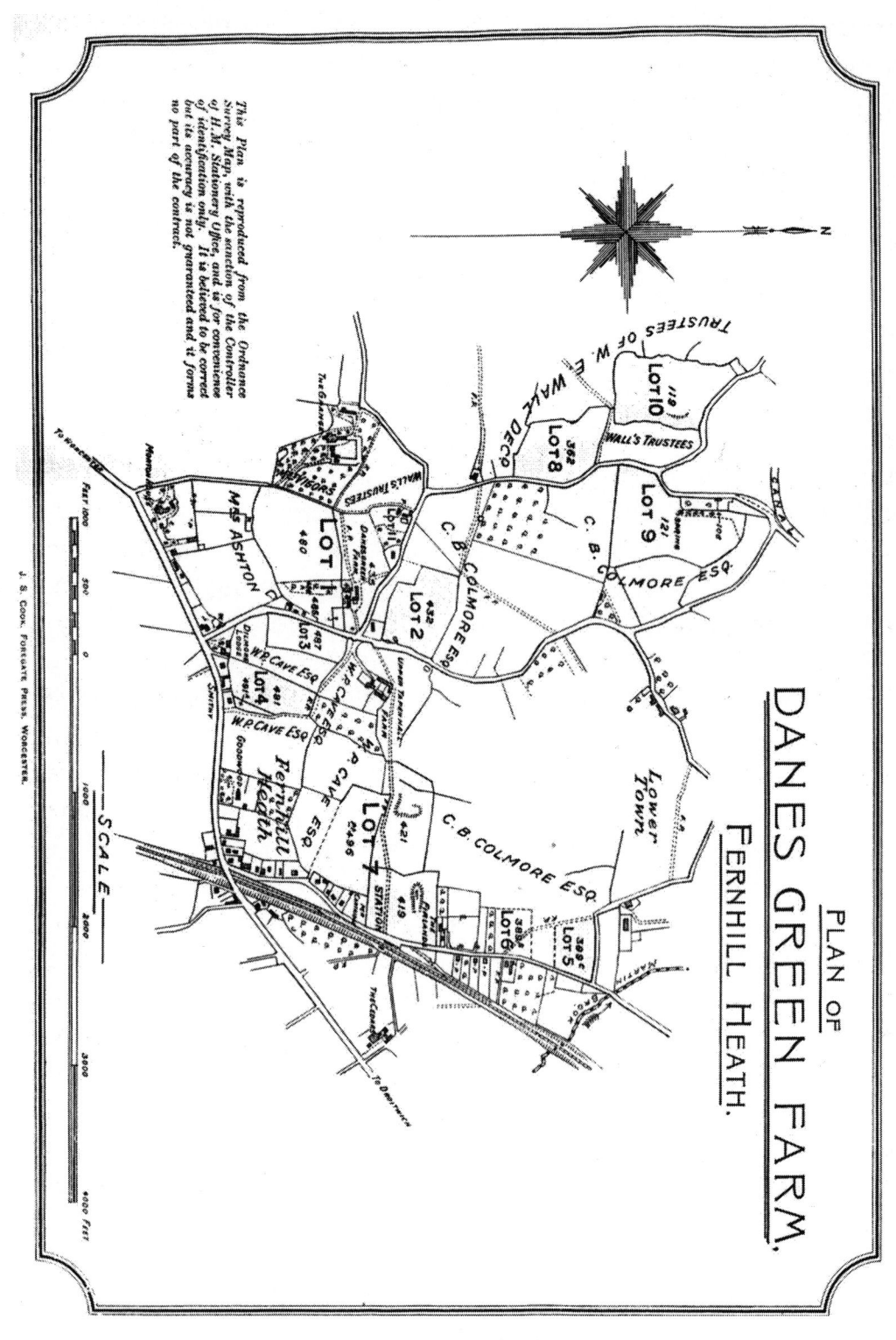

Fig 27. Danes Green Farm. Sale and Plan. 1918

the Droitwich Road, and land in Station Road were proposed and the latter was eventually selected. The building contractors, J. & A. Brazier Ltd., of Bromsgrove had won several contracts in Worcester to build council houses and were also used by Droitwich Rural District Council in 1928 to build six houses in Station Road, Nos. 77, 79, 81, 83, 85 and 87 at a cost of £2,521. 1s. 0d. (£2,521.5p).[6]

In 1931 the 3rd Lord Hindlip offered to sell the old brickyard in Hurst Lane for council houses, 2¼ acres for £100 plus all legal costs but his offer was refused, as the site was deemed unsuitable. A 1¼-acre site in Dilmore Lane was offered for sale at 1s.6d (7½p) per square yard to construct 10 council houses but both the Parish and District Councils considered the price too high. However, the District Council did eventually erect 12 council houses in Dilmore Lane which were completed in 1935, the price paid for the land and the cost of the houses were not disclosed. Allocation of housing was on the recommendation of the Parish Council with the Droitwich Rural District Council making the final decision, a practice that continued up until the abolition of the Droitwich Rural District Council in 1974.[7]

In September 1930 the Morton House Estate of 27 acres on Red Hill was sold.[8] Morton House became the new headquarters of the County Police. The land fronting the Droitwich Road on both the east and west was described as a suitable investment for housing, particularly as the price of building materials had fallen.

The private gated estate of Morton Avenue and Morton Road was built in 1934. Gates were erected off Droitwich Road and Dilmore Lane and closed every Good Friday to retain its private status. The roads were left unmade and without any paths. Towards the middle of Morton Road a gap was left open for potential development onto Danes Green Farm but the 1939-45 war put this on hold and it was not until 1999 that the farmland was eventually developed. In 1938 the row of detached houses and bungalows were built on the east side of Red Hill. At the same time the road was widened and improved and Red Hill was renamed Rose Mount and then Rose Bank.

---

[6] *Braziers, Builders of Bromsgrove. 1850-1990. Alan Richards.*
[7] *WRO. BA 10533/10.*
[8] *WRO. BA 5240/3.*

Fig 28. Road widening on Rose Bank and house building in progress. 1938.

From the late 1920s and during the 1930s detached, semi-detached homes and bungalows were built in Station Road and on the Droitwich Road. Several properties on the south side of the Droitwich Road beyond the railway bridge were large, detached and architecturally designed homes built for prosperous Worcester businessmen.

Droitwich Road
In 1926 the height of the road was raised, and again during the period of housing development in 1933 when it was heightened considerably between 18 inches and 2 feet. Surface water and flooding caused much damage to properties especially around Dilmore Lane where the problem was particularly aggravated. Eventually a drain was put in to take the excess rainwater and improve the drainage down Dilmore Lane.[9] The front garden of Pear Tree House is about 3 feet lower than the public

---

[9] *WRO. BA 4666.*

footpath. (The footpaths were put down later). At the entrance to 'The Brum' there is a long sloping path down onto the low-lying recreation ground. The ground floor of the 'Half Way House' was level with the road before the alterations.

Since the 1920s traffic had continued to increase through Fernhill Heath to and from Worcester and Droitwich. Car, motorbike and cycle ownership rose although there were still a great many horses and carts and horse riders. In 1924 there was talk of introducing a 20 mph speed limit through the village but no action was taken until 1935 when a 30 mph speed limit was proposed from the Worcester city boundary at Perdiswell to Hindlip Lodge, and eventually came into force in 1937 from the garage (now part of Stoneycroft Close) on the outskirts of the village to Hindlip Lodge only.[10]

New Water Supply and Sewage Disposal System

Simpkins & Lee of Fladbury, Near Pershore, and Clee & Son of Clerkenleap, Near Kempsey, built the Morton Avenue and Morton Road estate, and some of the houses were sold to investors who re-let them. The estate was without mains drainage or mains water, wells were sunk but not on every property, and before very long there were numerous complaints about them drying up. Some wells were dug deeper to obtain more water but a permanent solution had to be found not only on this new estate but also throughout Fernhill Heath. Droitwich Rural District Council wanted to expand its housing programme into the village but without a decent water supply this was not a viable exercise. Furthermore, there was great difficulty in providing an adequate water supply for fire fighting.

The Ministry of Health, the Worcestershire County Council and the Droitwich Rural District Council offered a grant of £700 each towards the cost of a new sewage scheme. Property owners were asked to contribute on the basis of £5 for a new house costing under £600 and £10 for a house over £600, which they refused to do.

A sewage scheme had been put forward as early as 1907 but the Worcestershire County Council and Droitwich Rural District Council after many years of negotiations were unable to purchase the land because the owner was asking too much and the scheme was eventually abandoned in 1913.

---

[10] *WRO. BA 10533/10.*

In July 1934 the County Medical Officer accompanied by the Sanitary Inspector of the Droitwich Rural District Council and the Chairman of the Parish Council surveyed the village with a view to supplying piped water to all properties and providing a new sewage disposal system. His report was damning.

The water supply was derived from wells, some 20 to 30 feet deep in the older part of the village. A few of the houses had hand-flushed water closets and cesspits in the gardens, but the majority had earth closets. Scavenging and excrement removal was undertaken weekly from 203 houses at an annual cost to the Rural District Council of £153, the contractor, Harry Farley, using a horse-drawn open dray for this purpose. The contents of a large square tank on the dray were tipped into a field on the other side of Martin Brook at the bottom of Station Road. It was alleged that the dray was used for other purposes too, such as the conveyance of fruit! It depended too, on which way the wind was blowing, as you could smell his approach some time before and for some time after he had gone. If there was no wind he was with you for the rest of the day! Most of the houses had a drain of some sort that was connected by lengths of sewer or road drains to the nearest brook or disposal sites at Sandyway, low lying swampy ground behind the 'White Hart', Martin Brook, and a ditch by the railway near to Spellis Cemetery.

The Medical Officer's opinion was that the existing arrangements were thoroughly bad. The practices contravened the existing law and constituted a menace to public health. He went on to recommend that a new system of piped water, new sewers and a proper method of sewage treatment should be provided. The Parish Council had already held a public meeting to discuss these proposals and 90% of the parishioners present were of the opinion that neither a public water supply nor a sewage disposal scheme were required for the village as the cost was likely to be borne by the ratepayers. It was not until 1938 that the two services were connected to the village, although not every property was immediately put on the sewer. The estimated cost of the water supply was £9,475 and the sewage disposal £15,580. The actual costs were £12,148 for the water supply and £19,000 for the sewage disposal.[11]

---

[11] WRO. BA 4666.

Royal Celebrations

The Silver Jubilee of King George V was celebrated in 1935 with Claines and Fernhill Heath holding separate events. There were church services, and later in the day sports for the children and all those under the age of 15 years were presented with a Jubilee mug.

The Revd C. Creighton and his son who resided at Tutnall House in Claines Lane offered a 7½-acre site opposite their home for a permanent recreation ground to be known as the 'George V Playing Fields'.

The Coronation of King George VI and Queen Elizabeth on the 12th May 1937, was celebrated with three separate events, one for Claines held in the field opposite Tutnall House, one for Fernhill Heath held in the vicinity of the 'Bull' and the 'White Hart' public houses and one for Fernhill Heath, Hindlip and Martin Hussingtree residents at Hindlip Stables, Pershore Lane, Martin Hussingtree.

Fig 29. Hindlip, Martin Hussingtree and Fernhill Heath residents outside Hindlip Stables. 1937.

Coronation of their Majesties King George VI & Queen Elizabeth

Celebrations at Fernhill Heath
NORTH CLAINES PARISH COUNCIL

WEDNESDAY, MAY 12th. 1937
"Coronation Day"

10-0 a.m.
Special Service in the Memorial Hall, the Rector, Rev. H. F. C. Balcomb.

1 p.m.
Cold Luncheon for Adults, men and women, over 60 years, who have given in their names, residing in Fernhill Heath (part of North Claines) will be provided FREE at the Bull Hotel, (by kind permission of Mr. and Mrs. J. Toppin). Beer, Tobacco, etc. will also be distributed, and also a TEA after the first part of the Sports in the afternoon.

2-30 p.m.
All school children who wish to come are asked to assemble near the Bull Hotel, and march to the Sports Ground with those taking part in the Comic Football Match (who will appear in their comic costumes) and those with Decorated Bicycles, etc. with the Band in attendance, to the Sports Ground, kindly lent for the Coronation occasion by Mr. Moorhouse.

The Committee trust that all parishioners will accept their hearty invitation to join in the procession for it is the National Rejoicing.

2-40 p.m.
Comic Football Match, all arrayed in various comic costumes—Mr. A. Mansell, referee—this will be well worth seeing. A very valuable cup will be presented to the winning team, who will be expected to retain it until the next Coronation. Prizes will also be awarded.

3-25 p.m.
Decorated Bicycle Parade. For the best decorated Bicycle. Prizes, 1st. 5/-, 2nd. 2/6, 3rd. 1/6. It is hoped that as many as possible will compete, so as to have a good show.

3-35 p.m.
Children's Races as per Programme.

Fig 30. Advertisement for Coronation of King George VI.

4 to 5 p.m.
   Children's Tea. Children will be entertained to a good tea at the Bull Hotel, when presents will be handed to each school child by the Committee, also prizes won at the Sports.

5 p.m. (approx.)
   A Meat Tea will be provided FREE to all ADULT Residents in Fernhill Heath at the Bull Hotel, who have received an invitation ticket, or, who have applied to the Hon. Secretary.

6-0 p.m.
   Sports for Adults (men and women) have been arranged as per Sports Programme. Winning competitors will be awarded their prizes after each event.

8 p.m.
   Social and Dance will be held in the Ballroom at the White Hart Hotel, by kind permission of Mr W. A. Smith, until 1 a.m. Admission will be FREE and a very special programme will be arranged, commencing with the CORONATION GRAND MARCH in which again, all must join for the National Rejoicing. The "Elite Band" will be in attendance from 2-0 p.m. to 1-0 a.m.

> *"And the day shall be filled with gladness,*
> *So put all your cares away,*
> *And join in our Celebrations,*
> *As Their Majesties wish you today."*

"GOD SAVE THE KING"

Mr. James Lane, (Chairman)   Mr. W. A. Crump (Hon. Sec.)   Mr. T. Wiggin (Hon. Treas.)

COMMITTEE

Mrs. T. Wiggin, Mrs. J. Toppin, Mrs. J. Fairbrother, Miss Gould, Mr. A. Grubb, Mr. A. Harris, Mr. W. Freeman, Mr. J. Ash, Mr. H. R. Lane, Mr. S. Lambert, Mr. J. Fairbrother, Mr. J. Clifford, Mr. J. Gould, Mr. A. Mansell, Mr. V. Wiggin, Mr. Ashmore, Mr. A. Mansell, (Junr.)
From whom any information will readily be given.

Will those Parishioners who have flags or any suitable decorations kindly give a good display on "Coronation Day."

In the event of a wet day, the Luncheon and Tea will be served for Adults, and Tea for the children, and also the Social and Dance in the evening will take place.

The Recreation ground

In 1931 Worcester city boundary was extended northwards taking in New Northwick, part of Cornmeadow Lane including the recreation ground owned by the Parish Council, and Perdiswell.[12] In 1935 The Revd Creighton had offered his piece of land in Claines Lane for use by North Claines residents. The price of the proposed recreation ground amounted to £1,400 which the Parish Council intended to buy by means of £900 of their own money and a £500 grant from the Ministry of Food & Fisheries, but on looking further into the matter the Deed of Gift expressly forbade holding sports, fetes or other entertainment for profit, and the Council pulled out of the talks.

The recreation ground in Cornmeadow Lane, Claines, was allocated to Worcester city in 1937 but was still owned by the Parish Council.[13]

With housing developments taking place in Dilmore and Fernhill Heath it was deemed more sensible to have a recreation ground in the northern part of the parish. Several residents came forward offering sites in Danes Green and at the bottom of Dilmore Lane but the prices were too high, £600 was asked for a piece of land on the west side of Dilmore Lodge but this was the wrong shape and size to permit or even make a football field. For some time Agatha, Lady Hindlip had allowed the village children to play on the old brickyard in Hurst Lane. The 3rd Lord Hindlip had died in December 1931, and Agatha, Lady Hindlip's agent was approached with a view to purchasing the site but she was only a tenant for life and unable to sell the land.

A field at Upper Tapenhall across to Station Road was considered but the cost was not to exceed £200 per acre, and a piece of land along the Wire Walk public footpath (from the station to Post Office Lane) was too near to the railway station. The Parish Council considered purchasing the bottom half of the Broom Meadows ('The Brum') but the owners refused to sell the land. Cadbury Brothers were also approached to sell a 4-acre site at Holy Claines Farm in Hindlip Lane.[14] Negotiations fell through because Cadbury's thought that their Blackpole factory would again be turned over for a munitions factory the same as the last war. In 1940 Mrs. Olive Miller of Rose Bank offered a piece of land behind Tapenhall House and, if taken up, she wanted the recreation ground to be known as 'The

---

[12] WRO. BA 4666.
[13] WRO. BA 4666.
[14] WRO. BA 4666.

Miller Playing Fields'. However, the land was needed for agricultural purposes during the war. Negotiations continued afterwards but she finally withdrew her offer in 1952.

World War II

Towards the end of the 1930s a decision was taken to build a dual carriageway off the Droitwich Road opposite Dilmore Lane, where there is a curved low wall with an entrance leading no-where, to take traffic down onto the Blackpole Lane. Cadbury Brothers, J. Archdale & Co. Ltd., and James Ward factories employed many people from Claines and Fernhill Heath. The two black and white Dilmore Cottages (now Dilmore Cottage) were to have been demolished to make way for the new road but World War II was declared on the 3rd September 1939 and the work was stopped.

Behind-the-scenes activities had been taking place for some time and both Oakfield House and Morton House on Rose Bank were requisitioned for the duration of the war. Oakfield was taken over first by The Royal Artillery and later as a hostel for the Women's Land Army drafted in to work on local farms, with the Ministry of Defence at Morton House. Nearby Hindlip Hall was requisitioned by the Ministry of Works in the event of evacuating the Air Defence Committee should the war take a turn for the worse. This did not happen and in 1940 the RAF 24 Group Technical Training Command took over the Hall. Agatha, Lady Hindlip continued to live there throughout the war and in 1946 moved to Fernhill Heath House.

ARP meetings were held and Mr. W. Woodhouse of Fernhill Heath became the first Chief Warden for the district followed by the Chief Constable, Captain Lloyd-Williams. The Memorial Hall became a First Aid Post with the District Nurse in attendance. The Local Defence Volunteers, later the Home Guard, was set up and Bob Carr of The Retreat, Fernhill Heath, handed out gas masks to local residents and those in Hindlip and Martin Hussingtree. As early as the 18th September 1939 he wrote to the local Worcester paper the 'Evening News & Times' warning readers about possible theft of leaving their gas masks on bicycles!

At the outbreak of World War II many farms were given over to pasture and cattle. The pasture was urgently needed for crops of corn, potatoes and fodder for cattle. A massive 'ploughing up' campaign began and farmers were offered a £2 incentive for any acre they ploughed up that had been grass for the past seven years, providing they did so by December 1939. The recreation ground in Cornmeadow Lane was ploughed up at this time.

In 1940 a 20 mph speed limit in darkness was introduced throughout the country in an attempt to combat the high incidence of road accidents. In the October the clocks did not go back one hour for wintertime, instead double summer time was introduced throughout the remainder of the war and reverted back to GMT in October 1946.

The only bombing raid in the Fernhill Heath area was on the afternoon of Wednesday, 14th August 1940, when eight heavy explosive bombs were dropped at Spellis Green, near Hindlip. There was slight damage to Spellis Farm (now The Bridges Restaurant) where the windows were blown in, and Tom and Gwen Griffiths's son, Gerald, who was looking out of the window at the time, was blown across the room. Tom came into the room with his dog and caught hold of his pet canary in its cage and without a word took them down into the cellar leaving Gwen and their children – Marina and Gerald, and their friend, Phyllis Jeffrey, to follow. They stayed down in the cellar until quite late. Spellis Cottages and Hurst Farmhouse were also slightly damaged. In an orchard above Hurst Farmhouse a fruit dealer called Mr. Bishop, who was elderly and stone-deaf, and a young lad, John Saunders, were picking plums. The plane came overhead and the horse with the dray bolted but the old man went on picking plums not having heard a thing! John Saunders was terrified but unharmed.

The pilot was heading for Cadbury Brothers factory at Blackpole, requisitioned again for the duration of the war as a munitions factory. At the last moment he decided not to bomb the factory and ditched them in the nearby fields. Rumours were rife that the pilot was a former pupil of Malvern Boys' College and knew the area well.

On the opposite side of the junction to where the 'White Hart' public house stands was Perry's sweets and fancy goods shop. In 1941 the shop was pulled down to make way for a new road down to Blackpole. Up until then there had only been a cart track to Hurst Farm where a gate led through onto a path that went down to Spellis Green, but cyclists and motorcyclists began using the track as a short cut down to Blackpole instead of Hindlip Lane. The new road, Hurst Lane, did not go straight down to Blackpole as it does today, but went as far as Spellis Green turned left along the front of Spellis Cottages and then into Blackpole Road.

Fig 31. Fernhill Heath Home Guard

The Ministry of Agricultural and Fisheries was empowered to set up County War Agricultural Committees and these were given authority to increase food production. National Farm Surveys of England and Wales were carried out during 1940-1943.The first Survey was to direct another 'ploughing-up' campaign under which large expanses of grassland were prepared for cultivation. It was vital to assess the ability of each farmer to play his part in the national food production plan. Claines Survey was carried out in 1941 and included in Fernhill Heath, were The Cedars, Fernhill Heath House, The Gables, Oakfield House and the Worcestershire Hunt, with the surrounding farms; The Grange, Danes Green Farm, Upper Tapenhall, Tapenhall, Hurst Farm and Spellis Farm.

Some of the farms were run down through lack of money and shortage of labour.[15]

A regulation was brought in during 1941 that anyone who had a spare room war workers or evacuees could be billeted with them. The village took in many of them, relatives and strangers, sometimes there were two families living in one small house. Government money was received to give the evacuee children a treat but any funds likely to be given for another similar event would be put aside and used as a Boot and Clothing Fund.

Throughout the war the Memorial Hall held regular dance nights, a welcome relief to forget the war for a few hours. Dances were held to raise money for the war effort. In May 1944 a Youth Group Dance was held to raise money in conjunction with the County Salute Weeks Droitwich Campaign, "Salute the Soldier" to the Worcestershire Regiment. The District target was £125,000.

Housing developments

At the end of the war some of the evacuees and Land Army girls decided to settle in the village because they had met local young men and women and wanted to settle down here. There was an acute shortage of houses and in 1947 council houses were built in Station Road and Kennels Lane.

The development of Dilmore began in the late 1940s with houses built in and behind Dilmore Lane. The new roads were called Dilmore Avenue and Tapenhall Road. Under Government ruling the developer could only sell the houses built in Dilmore Lane. Houses built in Dilmore Avenue and Tapenhall Road were council-rented accommodation.

Tapenhall was about ½ mile away from the village shops and post office. The only shops in the vicinity were at the bottom of Morton Avenue and from Ted Palmer who sold sweets and cigarettes from a conservatory built on the side of his home at Dilmore Cottages on the Droitwich road.

The next phase of development on Dilmore came in the early 1950s.

---

[15] *National Archives. WO 363/5.96.*

Fig 32. Dilmore Cottages 1952.

Chapter 5
1951-2000

There were a great many changes throughout this period beginning with further development on Dilmore and the possibility of a replacement Hindlip School. The Parish Council continued its search for a suitable recreation ground. In the 1960s the opening of the M5 motorway and the A449 Northern Link took traffic away from the busy Droitwich Road through the village and the railway station closed. With inflation running high in the 1970s and 80s attempts were made to get the railway station re-opened. The last decade of the 20th century brought more housing developments to the village.

Railway Accident

The only rail accident that occurred locally was on the morning of the 2nd January 1951 when the 6.33 am Worcester to Birmingham passenger train crashed into a goods train carrying 30 trucks of sugar beet. The goods train had been reversing into what is known as a refuge siding and was nearly clear of the main line when it was run into by the passenger train. Fortunately there were no serious injuries to the passengers. The two train crews were slightly injured and taken to hospital but were discharged after treatment.

The engines of both trains were turned on their sides and lay on the lines just short of the platform on the Worcester side of the line. The lines were completely blocked and breakdown vans were rushed to the scene. During the hours the lines were blocked single-decker buses were specially chartered to take passengers to Droitwich Station though the buses found progress difficult as six inches of snow lay on the ground. The collision was apparently deadened by the snowfall so that residents in the immediate vicinity did not hear it. By daylight the wrecked engines could be seen from the railway bridge.[1]

---

[1] *Worcester Evening News & Times. 2nd January 1951.*

The Three Counties Agricultural Show

Every year the Three Counties Agricultural Society held a show in rotation at Gloucester, Worcester and Hereford. In June 1952 the show was held at Hindlip Park with access onto the showground at Sandyway. It was an exciting time for residents who watched the preparations for this event and were able to visit the show so close by. On the first day a colourful opening ceremony took place at noon with a procession of Mayors and Corporations of the three Counties and the Lord Mayor of Birmingham who were met by the Show President. There were over 400 trade exhibits, including local businesses, illustrating the modern trends in agriculture and horticulture with nearly ¾ mile of up-to-date machinery, numerous new inventions and developments. On the third and final day the show closed with a ceremonial parade by the Worcestershire Regiment. The show was held again in Hindlip Park in 1955 and the attendance figure reached nearly 46,000 over the three days. The traffic coming out of the showground was so heavy that there was a 3-mile hold-up to Worcester.[2] The Show Committee realized that a permanent site would have to be found for this popular event and in 1958 the show opened on its present site at Malvern.

Coronation Celebrations

The Coronation of HM Queen Elizabeth II on the 2nd June 1953 brought another happy and festive occasion to the village. The day was one of two days' public holiday and the ecclesiastical parish of Hindlip and Martin Hussingtree celebrated the Coronation with a fancy dress parade from the 'White Hart' public house to a meadow in Sling Lane led by the Coronation Queen, Irene Abrahams and her two attendants, Marilyn Price and Margaret Ash. Eileen Mann was Hindlip School's Coronation Queen with Barry Parker as the Duke of Edinburgh.

During the afternoon there were sports and a comic football match between Hindlip County Police HQ and Hindlip Football Club, and every child was given a ¼ lb bag of sweets. Teas were provided for every child and adult. Children under 15 were given a Coronation mug. In the Memorial Hall 80 old people sat down to tea, and afterwards the ladies were presented with a packet of tea and the men with tobacco. The children from the Baptist Chapel entertained them with country dancing.[3]

---

[2] *Worcester Evening News & Times.* 9th June 1952.
[3] *Worcester Evening News & Times.* 4th June 1953.

Fig 33. Eileen Mann, Hindlip School Coronation Queen. 1953

Public Houses

The hey-day of the village pubs was in the 1950s and early 1960s before the opening of the M5 motorway. At weekends and Bank Holidays coach parties stopped off either at the 'Live and Let Live' or the 'White Hart' for a drink on their way home after a day's outing. With the larger car park there could be as many as 12 coaches visiting the 'Live and Let Live' that brought in between four and five hundred people. Back in May 1948 a new bowling green had opened behind the public house, and later, Agatha, Lady Hindlip gave a pavilion, a wartime surplus American prefab, from Hindlip Hall. In 1954 the Holt Brewery, part of Ansells Brewery, applied to Droitwich Rural District Council to erect an assembly room and a bowling pavilion on part of the children's play area within the grounds of the public house. Permission was only given for the pavilion that could be used to provide teas for the Bowling Club.

Sometimes there were scenes of drunkenness and fighting outside the public houses, and one man died as a result of fighting outside the 'White Hart' on a Saturday night and his body was found the next morning lying near the railway line below the public house.

Dances were held at the Memorial Hall every Saturday night and during the interval, as no alcohol was served on the premises, some of the dancers would pop along to the pubs and then back again to the dance. Late night buses to Worcester and Droitwich took the revellers home. Dances were also held in the Assembly Room at the rear of the 'White Hart'. One long time resident remarked, "This was where the posh people went to dance!" Use of this building gradually declined and in 1968 was last used as auction rooms by a Worcester estate agent before it was demolished to make way for a larger car park.

New Housing, proposed new Hindlip School and recreation facilities

By 1953 there were over 80 people on the council house waiting list for homes in the village. The Droitwich Rural District Council put forward a scheme to develop 13½ acres of land on Tapenhall Farm. 6½ acres of land providing sites for 52 houses and the remaining 7 acres for a replacement Hindlip School on 'The Brum'. The Parish Council approached the Local Education Authority suggesting that a portion of the 7 acres could be used as a recreation ground, but the LEA was only prepared to release 2 acres, which were not enough.[4] Dilmore Avenue was extended and the council flats and two shops to serve the area were built, but only one shop opened. Council houses were erected in Cresswell Close and named after the former headmaster of Claines School and parish councillor, James Cresswell. The school was not built.

There was surplus land at the rear of the flats in Dilmore Avenue (now garages and Lane House) that the Parish Council thought might be possible to lease for a small playground and to erect a hut for use as a Community Centre. The new Dilmore residents formed themselves into a group and began fund raising for this venture, as grants were available. The Parish Council eventually decided not to negotiate for the land and in 1956 the group disbanded. However, the Parish Council continued looking for a piece of ground to purchase and applied to Droitwich Rural District Council for permission to use a piece of land in Kennels Lane but was refused. Agreement was finally reached in 1959 for the sale of the recreation ground in Cornmeadow Lane, Claines, and was sold to Worcester City Council for £1,600 with a condition that the proceeds of the sale must be vested in another one.

In the early 1960s further development took place on Dilmore providing three council-owned blocks of flats; The Meadows, Lane House and Preston Court. The latter two were named after two former parish councillors, James Lane and C. G. Preston. Police houses were built in Dilmore Avenue. Private houses were built in Shrawley Road, Perrycroft Close, Broom Meadow Road, Broadfield Crescent and Eastfield Close. Off Station Road in Firlands Close and Kennels Lane. Also in Ivy Lane. With this large housing development and an increase in the number of families with children of school age there was again the possibility of the Worcestershire County Council providing a new school but this was deferred until 1972.[5]

The 1960s brought several changes both in and around the village.

---

[4] WRO. BA 10533/1.
[5] WRO. BA 10533/2.

Agatha, Lady Hindlip

In 1962 Agatha, Lady Hindlip died. For many years she had lived at Fernhill Heath House and had taken a keen interest in village life. She had been one of the managers of Hindlip School. In 1949 she had instigated the formation of the Red Cross Club in Fernhill Heath for persons then over 65 years of age and became their first Chairman. For a number of years she had been an active member of the British Red Cross Society and in 1953 received the Coronation Medal for her services to that organisation. She had also worked closely with the City and County Nursing Association its chief function prior to the National Health Service was to raise funds for the payment of district nurses, to provide them with cars or motorcycles.

After her death in 1962 part of the Hindlip Estate comprising of 23 lots were auctioned at the Winter Gardens, Droitwich, in July 1963. The sale included Fernhill Heath House with a gardener's cottage, 16 cottages, a shop, the old post office, several pieces of land and allotments.

M5 Motorway and the Northern Link

Retirement of some of the local shopkeepers and the opening of supermarkets in Worcester and Droitwich coincided with many more residents owning cars who travelled out of the village to do their shopping.

As far back as 1944 a national motorway had already been partly planned from Birmingham to Bristol to take the traffic, especially heavy vehicles, away from the main roads and cities. In the early 1960s traffic from Worcester to Droitwich would be bumper to bumper through the village on Bank Holiday evenings. On the 20th July 1962 the M5 motorway opened. Access onto Junction 6 at Warndon was via Pershore Lane at Martin Hussingtree. Soon after the opening of the M5 work began on the new Northern Link from Junction 6 to the A449 Ombersley Road at Bevere. Hurst Lane was altered near Hurst Farm with slip roads onto/off the new link road, at Spellis Green the cottages now overlook the Northern Link and part of the old Blackpole Road was used as a slip road onto/off the new link road. A new bridge was built taking Hurst Lane straight into the upgraded Blackpole Road. Part of Hindlip Lane near Spellis Farm (now the Bridges Restaurant) was used for the new link road and a new section of Hindlip Lane was built on the other side of Spellis Farm. On the 12th April 1965 the Northern Link opened.

At first it seemed that the planners had got it wrong as the link road was very little used and would become a white elephant! Local estate agents began promoting this new road when advertising village homes 'as near to the M5 motorway' attracting commuters into the village who worked away from the area.

Droitwich Road

The vexed question of speed limits was again raised in the 1960s with a proposal to abolish the 30 mph speed limit from Timbers Garage (now part of Stoneycroft Close) to Hindlip Lodge gates, and a counter proposal to increase the limit to 40 mph in a restricted zone in the village itself. In 1963 the Ministry of Transport introduced a speed limit of 40 mph from Timbers Garage to Hindlip Lodge.[6]

After a fatal road accident in the village in 1974 a public meeting was held to discuss the traffic speeding through the village. Feelings ran high and the village area was dubbed 'Murder Mile'. An action group was formed to try to reduce the 40 mph speed limit to 30 mph and to install a pelican crossing near the village shops and, the then local Member of Parliament, Peter Walker, was brought into the discussions. Neither the proposed speed reduction nor the pelican crossing met with the Ministry of Transport's criteria. This decision did not deter the action group and in 1980 they presented a petition to the Ministry of Transport with over 200 signatures for a crossing. In May 1982 they were informed that theirs was a borderline case. Eventually in 1986 a pelican crossing was installed near the village shops.[7]

The Cedars

In 1967 The Cedars, the large mansion house on the Droitwich Road opposite the Memorial Hall was demolished to make way for Droitwich Rural District Council's sheltered housing project for the elderly. Severnminster Developments Ltd won the contract. At the same time Severnminster had received planning permission to build private houses on two fields off Post Office Lane. Development commenced and it soon became apparent that houses were being erected over the public footpath known as the Wire Walk leading from the former railway station to Post

---

[6] WRO. BA 4666.
[7] WRO. BA 11747/1.

Office Lane. Most of the old footpath was lost except for a small section between Nos.17 and 19 Fir Tree Road. A Public Inquiry was held in the Memorial Hall and on the recommendation of the Planning Inspector the path was re-routed from the former railway station through Yew Tree Lane, into Fir Tree Road, between Nos. 17 and 19, into Pine Close and onto Post Office Lane. Severnminster Developments later went into receivership with the majority of the houses, bungalows, and 60% of the sheltered housing complex unfinished. 'The Cedars' sheltered housing was completed and opened in 1970.

New Telephone Exchange
A new £151,000 telephone exchange in Dilmore Lane was opened in 1969 to provide a service for up to 13,000 subscribers.

Proposed new Hindlip School and recreation facilities
In September 1968 over 100 residents signed a petition asking for a recreation ground in the Dilmore area. The following March the Parish Council began leasing 'The Brum' as a recreation ground from the County Education Committee whilst efforts continued to find a permanent site to purchase. A site was looked at in Post Office Lane in 1972 but was too expensive and the 4th Lord Hindlip was not prepared to sell a piece of land opposite Fernhill Heath House.

Another possible site for a recreation ground was a 6-acre meadow behind Station Road with access from the bottom of Northfield Close. This site caused so much dissension with local residents that they organised themselves into several action groups to fight the proposal. A counter action group was formed in favour of the proposed site. The arguments continued for several years and in 1980 a Parish Poll was held at which two thirds of the parish voted, resulting in a small majority against purchasing the field. A second Parish Poll in 1981 resulted in an overwhelming majority against the purchase of the site particularly at a time of high inflation when no one wanted to see a rate increase.

The lease on 'The Brum' expired in March 1983 because the site was due to be developed as a replacement for Hindlip School. The Parish Council had looked into the possibility of renting a room in the village to use as a parish room, they then agreed to a joint partnership with Hereford & Worcester County Council with provision for such a room, a hall for use by the school and public, together with a playing field/recreation ground within the new school premises. At an open meeting held at Hindlip School those present voted against a new school preferring the old school building to be upgraded. The building of a new school was put back to 1986/87, but of course, has never been built.

The Parish Council continued leasing 'The Brum' and a fete was held on 'The Brum' in August 1983 with funds raised going towards a Community Centre. Fetes were held again in 1984, 1985 and 1986 and then abandoned. The council has continued leasing 'The Brum' and providing play equipment for the village children.

Housing developments

House building slowed down during the 1970s due to high inflation, with only small developments built; The Goodwood Green development of Epsom Close, Ascot Close and Goodwood Close opened up the last section of Dilmore Avenue into Shrawley Road. New houses were built off Post Office Lane.

Fernhill Heath Railway Station

Under the 'Beeching Axe' the station had closed on 5th April 1965, although it was not until Sunday, 1st November 1970 that the signal box was demolished to make way for a new footbridge replacing the footway across the railway line.

In 1975 the Parish Council approached British Rail asking them to consider re-opening the station in conjunction with BR's 'Save Energy' Campaign as many residents worked in Birmingham, Worcester and further afield and wanted to commute by train because of the ever-increasing cost of petrol. Their request was turned down. In March 1981 British Rail was again approached, and replied that to re-open the station with two platforms would cost over £80,000 and neither they nor Hereford & Worcester County Council had enough money to finance the project, and secondly, there was a lack of car parking space. A third and final attempt was made in 1987 without success.[8]

---

[8] *WRO. BA 10533/2.*

Fig 34. Signal box and new footbridge.

Twinning

A trend began in the late 1970s for cities and towns to twin with our European neighbours. Villages followed suit, and Fernhill Heath was no exception and two villages in France were contacted, Carteret and St. Hilaire-la-Palud. Only St. Hilaire responded. A public meeting was held in June 1984 and a visit was made, followed by a return visit in October. Interest in the twinning began to wane and the idea was dropped.[9]

Re-development of Preston's Garage and the old Bakery

In 1988 Keephill Cottage at the rear of Preston's Garage together with the garage and car showroom near the junction with Hurst Lane were demolished to make way for Berkeley Gardens, a development of several large detached houses and bungalows. At the same time the antiques

---

[9] WRO. BA 11747/1.

shop, formerly Baylis's bakery and grocery shop, closed and was converted into several properties.

Fig 35. Preston's Garage sold on the 18th July 1988 for re-development.

New developments, Stoneycroft Close and Balmoral Close

Stoneycroft Cottage had been built many years ago on a large plot of land on the Droitwich Road. After the last owner died the site became derelict. In 1988 this site together with the car showroom on the adjoining land were cleared and demolished to make way for a new development of 33 houses on Stoneycroft Close. In 1989 Bryant Homes built Balmoral Close, a detached estate of 34 homes on an old orchard at the bottom of Station Road opposite Kennels Lane.

Further expansion of Fernhill Heath

Every decade since the 1920s new houses had been built and by 1990 there were nearly 1,000 properties with a population of 4,000+ in Fernhill Heath. Over the past few years some residents thought that the village offered very few amenities and had pressed for the re-opening of the railway station, a by-pass, a new village hall, a chemist's shop, a doctor's surgery and a recreation ground.

In 1990 Hereford & Worcester County Council published their County Structure Plan setting out the County's housing and employment needs, shopping, recreation and open spaces up to 2001. Following the Structure Plan came Wychavon District Council's Local Plan with Droitwich requiring 4,500 new homes either within the town or the surrounding villages. Fernhill Heath with a good infrastructure and access to the M5 motorway was deemed suitable to provide 150 new dwellings, much to the dismay of many residents. The number was later reduced to 95 and then to 50 by 1992. The preferred site was the former 'Live and Let Live' public house that had closed in the late 1980s and the bowling green some years earlier, together with a piece of land to the rear.

Local landowners and outside developers began taking an interest in Fernhill Heath and put forward several potential sites with promises to improve village amenities:-

1. Danes Green Farm on the outskirts of the village.
2. Land opposite Fernhill Heath House.
3. Post Office Lane.
4. O'Keys Farm.
5. East of Hurst Lane.
6. West of Station Road.
7. Land on the Droitwich Road opposite Dilmore Lane junction fronting the A38 and behind.
8. Pool House. Alongside the railway off Hurst Lane incorporating a railway halt with platforms on both sides of the track, a park and ride terminal and a development of 80 homes.
9. Land at the rear of Station Road, Kennels Lane and across to Lower Town for some 550 homes including provisions for social housing, landscaped open spaces, recreation areas, a medical centre with a chemist's shop, a village hall, a contribution to schools and reinstatement of the railway station with a park and ride car park. Access would be via an improved Dilmore Lane with a new roundabout at the A38 junction.
10. The former 'Live and Let Live' public house and bowling green and land to the rear.

A Green Belt had already been drawn up around the village to protect the countryside and to stop coalescence between settlements.

The battle to stop so much possible development in the village began with residents in Post Office Lane forming themselves into an action group that prevented 75 houses being built on land off Post Office Lane.

A public meeting was held in the Memorial Hall at which over 300 residents attended. Another residents' action group was set up who put forward 'The Community Plan' proposing a longer term housing plan up to 2025.

A Public Inquiry was held in 1993 to consider the District Council's Local Plan at which developers and residents put forward their views. The outcome of the Inquiry was a large increase in the number of new homes to 200 to be built on three sites. The 'Live and Let Live' 50 houses, Danes Green Farm 120 houses and Station Road 30 houses.

The former 'Live and Let Live' site was developed by Walton Homes in 1999 with 32 private houses and bungalows and social housing, and named Agatha Gardens after the late Agatha, Lady Hindlip. Ivy Lane was slightly altered with a new access off Agatha Gardens and a grassed area between the lane and the Droitwich Road complimented the new estate. In the same year development began on Danes Green Farm.

A number of houses were also built in the village on 'windfall sites'; large back gardens that owners no longer wanted.

Fernhill Heath Railway Bridge

In March 1994 the railway bridge was badly damaged by a burst water main and the Droitwich Road was closed to traffic[10] and re-opened in May to single line traffic only. The Department of Transport held an exhibition in the Baptist Church hall setting out their answer to the problem, which was to infill the outer arches of the old bridge and reinforce the centre arch with a concrete slab. The cost of the scheme amounted to £500,000 of which £150,000 was for a temporary bridge and £350,000 to repair the main bridge. At the end of October work began on building the temporary bridge with a walkway alongside the main bridge, and work began on the main bridge in the New Year with traffic crossing over the temporary bridge. The bridge was repaired and a new road surface laid down and

---

[10] *Worcester Evening News. 5th March 1994.*

the bridge re-opened on the 16th June only to be closed to traffic the following day as the new road surface was not up to standard and had to be replaced. Finally the road was opened and traffic began to flow through the village once again and village life returned to normal.[11]

Village Fetes

Two very successful fetes were held in the field below Pool House (now demolished), in 1999 and 2000. All monies raised were given to local charities.

---

[11] *Worcester Evening News. 18th June 1995.*

Chapter 6
The Workhouse

Following the Dissolution of the Monasteries (1536-39) the responsibility of looking after the poor and sick fell to the parish churches. In 1597-98 an Act was passed that enabled parishes to levy a poor rate and paupers were provided with relief, either 'indoor' for those maintained in a poor house or 'outdoor' for those in their own home.

The Poor Law Act of 1601 brought in regulations that remained in use for the next two centuries and Overseers of the Poor were appointed at the annual Vestry Meetings. The Law of Settlement Act of 1662 empowered the Overseers of the Poor to remove any strangers from the parish who did not obtain work within 40 days and who did not rent property worth £10. A stranger could claim settlement in the parish after 40 days and once granted a settlement certificate could claim poor relief.

Claines Church possessed several charities that were used throughout the year towards rents, clothing, fuel and bread to alleviate the suffering of the poor. In the early part of the 20th century these charities were grouped together to form the Claines United Charities. In 1736 Mary Walker, who had lived at Tutnall, in her will bequeathed the rent from two cottages and gardens in Deans Green (Danes Green) to purchase four gowns for four poor widows with any money left over to be used in the distribution of bread.[1] Her brother, William Norton of Hawford, was another benefactor.

In 1856 the Charity Commissioners gave the Vestry permission to sell the two cottages but they then decided to retain them and were eventually sold in 1974.

From the early 18th century the population of Claines increased considerably especially in the urban area of Whistone, elsewhere in the manor the population was low. An assessment made in 1747 of those eligible to pay the Poor Rate levy in Tapenhall tithing found only 33 householders. From 1746 to 1795 many of the poor were farmed out to Robert Tasker who had set up a workhouse in St. Peter the Great, Worcester.[2] In 1788 a Mr. Yeoman wrote to the Bishop of Worcester

---

[1] WRO. BA 2683/2.
[2] WRO. BA 2683/21 (iii).

asking for permission to enclose 17 acres of land on Vernal Heath on which to build a workhouse but was refused consent.[3]

Fig 36. Thatch Cottage, formerly two cottages owned by Mary Walker who bequeathed the rents to Claines Church in 1736.

For some years a house adjoining the clerk's house in Claines churchyard had been converted into six tenements for the poor but by 1796 was in such a bad state of repair that the Vestry had to decide whether to repair or demolish it. Plans and estimates were obtained to build twelve houses but due to overspending of the poor rate levy the houses were neither repaired nor rebuilt. Again Mr. Yeoman approached the Bishop suggesting enclosure of the Heath and alleging that Mr. Ellis who lived opposite the church did not want to see the old tenements rebuilt as they interfered with the view from his home!

The whole of the country suffered disastrously from poor harvests in 1794 and 1795 and several severe winters followed. The continuing war with France affected the cost of imported corn and the cost of bread soared. In 1795 the Speenhamland (Near Newbury, Berks) system was

---

[3] *WRO. BA 2636/138.*

introduced and this actively encouraged employers to reduce wages knowing that parishes would make up the difference. The poor rate levy was calculated at two-thirds the value of property and collected on property worth more than £10 per annum twice yearly. In Claines the parishioners who paid this levy and other taxes including land tax, window tax and a registration tax on baptisms, marriages and burials, complained that many of those out of work were idlers who wanted to live off the parish. There was a significantly large increase in the expenditure of relief to the poor and the accounts were considerably overdrawn for some years as a large percentage of labourers lived in a state of abject poverty. Some of the Vestry members formed themselves into a committee to assist the Overseers of the Poor and each member was allotted a particular area of the parish. John Copson, the tenant of Puck Pit Farm, was allotted Tapenhall, and details of any persons in need of relief were passed to the Overseers. At this time too, very few servants lived in, and the degrading practice of 'roundsmen' was introduced with the unemployed poor going round the local tradesmen and farmers begging for work.

Poor children above 8 years old were immediately put out as apprentices and bound by an indenture to occupiers of houses and/or occupiers of land for 21 years. Those children whose premiums were paid for by charity were sent out of the parish. They would then gain the right of settlement in the parish where they served their apprenticeship.

Agricultural labourers' wages in 1796 were 7s per week for those living in, and 9s per week for those who lived out.

In 1800 the price of bread was so high that the poor were unable to purchase their staple diet and rioting took place in Worcester with the Militia called out to quell the crowds.

In 1804 the six tenements for the poor in Claines churchyard were demolished and twelve almshouses were erected.

John Copson of Puckpit Farm and a former Steward of the Manorial Courts died in 1807 leaving just £20. His will reflects that times were hard for tenant farmers too. He held a freehold and copyhold estate in Claines called Bomfords (location unknown) mortgaged at £350, three copyhold estates in Claines, and had intended giving his daughter £200.[4]

---

[4] WRO. BA 8782/76 (6).

A decision was taken in 1809 that a workhouse should be provided either by building or renting a place for the maintenance and employment of the poor. Nothing came of this decision. In 1811 the Vestry passed another resolution to provide a workhouse. A house owned by Claines Church situated in Ombersley Road, Worcester, and occupied by John Burt, was thought to be suitable and plans and estimates were drawn up and put forward but the scheme was abandoned in early 1812.

At the April meeting of 1812 the Vestry resolved to erect a new workhouse in open countryside on the Droitwich Road at Fearnall Heath providing the Bishop of Worcester would permit the enclosure of about 4 acres of land and grant a lease to the parish officers in trust for the use of the parish. Within a month the Bishop had allowed a piece of land on the Heath to be used. An advertisement placed in the local paper required estimates for posts and rails for the boundary fencing, the land properly levelled and trenched 14 to 16 inches deep with a ditch sunk around the boundary. Joseph Freeman agreed to do the work for 2s.6d per perch by the 20th June. The land was then limed and sown with turnips. A further

Fig 37. The former Workhouse, Droitwich Road.

advertisement was placed asking for plans and estimates and a tender for £700 was accepted to build a workhouse for 40 persons. The final cost of the workhouse was £750. Several landowners advanced money for the building in shares of one of £100 and two of £50 with a dividend fixed annually without the deduction of the property expenses. The cost of fitting out the workhouse with beds and bedding, clothes, furniture and food was borne by the ratepayers.

By April 1813 the workhouse was nearly finished and fit for habitation and Luke Russell was appointed governor for one year being allowed for each man, woman and child 4s.6d per week for 12 persons, above that number 5s.0d per week. For the aged and infirmed not able to work 3s.6d per week. He was entitled to use the land belonging to the workhouse and lived rent-free.

Within two months of the workhouse opening it was not filled to capacity and Warndon parish was invited to send some of their poor to Fearnall Heath paying £20 and finding all the bedsteads, sheets and blankets, and paying the governor an annual sum mutually agreed. By 1815 the parishes of Martin Hussingtree, which had its own workhouse, Crowle, Salwarpe, Himbleton and Tibberton all paid an annual charge of between £12 and £15 to the Vestry to send their poor to the workhouse providing there was enough room for the Claines paupers.

In March 1816 Luke Russell left and William Green was appointed governor. His allowance for children above 7 years old was 3s.6d and under 7 years 3s.0d. Women lying-in 10s.0d and no allowance given until children were a month old. All poor children of 9 years old and upward were put out as apprentices. All assessable property in the parish was re-valued and a higher levy introduced.

The 22-year war with France ended in 1815 but peace was marred by general distress and discontent affecting both the agricultural and manufacturing interests of the country. There was heavy taxation and stagnation of trade. Other nations had begun to manufacture their own goods and the demand for English goods had dwindled. The Corn Law Act was passed forbidding the importing of foreign corn unless the price of wheat rose to 80 shillings a quarter. This law caused much concern among farmers who recommended a decrease in the burden of taxation.

There were bad harvests for several years and during 1818 work became so scarce that all farm labourers were discharged who did not belong to the parish and were returned to their own under the Act of Settlement. Only those born in the parish were entitled to obtain work. Those unable to find farm work were employed in the local gravel pits or sent out as roundsmen to find work with the landowners. Anyone who refused to comply with the regulations was reported to the Overseers. Rents that had been paid by the Overseers were stopped in 1819 and any paupers applying for rent was refused and a place in the workhouse was, for some, the only option. The parish hired out the able-bodied paupers and retained any wages earned in return for their maintenance. Many paupers refused to enter the workhouse and encroached upon the waste or heath land at Fearnall Heath erecting makeshift shelters, but were not forced to take them down. It is a fallacy to believe that a squatter could obtain squatters' rights if he built a cottage in a day with the smoke coming out of the chimney by the evening. These paupers had no money to buy any building materials and to steal could result in transportation, imprisonment or hanging. The lord of the manor compromised by building small copyhold cottages on the heath and accepting a rent from them of 1s 0d or 2s 0d per annum.

The squatters were also liable to pay an annual sum of 30s.0d per acre to the Overseers of the Poor. Agricultural workers' wages averaged then between 9s and 10s per week.

In the spring of 1821 the workhouse was re-organised providing employment, and the following year a Steale Mill and dressing machine were bought in order to employ the able-bodied inmates in grinding and dressing wheat.

All properties were again assessed during the years 1822-3 and two thirds of the parish contributed towards the poor rate.

In 1826 the Worcester gloving trade was dealt a heavy blow by the repeal of import duty on foreign goods and suffered badly from the depression and many outworkers lost their jobs.

The Vestry agreed in 1826 that the workhouse, although it had served its purpose well in providing for the poor, was a liability on the parish. The workhouse had originally cost £750 but £625 was still owed to the shareholders, added to this were further varying sums of dividends amounting to £112. 7. 6d owed to them. The Vestry resolved that the shareholders would all be legally paid out of the poor rates immediately after the workhouse expenditure had been met. However, they were unable to clear the debt and the following year a decision was taken that it would be better to provide for the poor without the provision of a workhouse. The paupers were removed and sought parish relief, but some were homeless. The beds and bedding were removed from the workhouse and given to the needy. The Vestry now had to consider renting a house, and in 1828 went back to leasing the workhouse in Fearnall Heath at a rent of £35 per annum. A surgeon and apothecary were appointed with Samuel Parry as governor at £45 per annum. Within a month there were problems and Samuel Parry, several years later, was called before a Vestry meeting to bring them the money he had received from the crops, gravel and stone he had disposed of, and to inform them of the fixtures left in the house at the time the workhouse was vacated. Later in 1828 the Vestry decided that the old workhouse and land was of no benefit to the parish whatsoever but another property would have to be found. They approached both Hallow and Ombersley parishes to see whether they would admit the Claines poor, and Ombersley was prepared to admit some at a lower rate than Hallow. Eventually in January 1830 a house and an acre of land owned by William Wall was found in Claines Lane (in the vicinity of the present-day Institute and Vicarage) and rented on a three-year lease at £27 per annum. The Assistant Overseer of the Poor, R. T. Jackson, resided in the house and took on the responsibility of farming out the poor and providing sufficient maintenance for every person sent to the poor house at 4s.0d per week per head above 5 years old, and 3s.0d per week per head under 5 years old, and 10s. 0d for the lying-in month for every poor woman, any poor child born in the house not to be paid for until one month old then at 3s.0d per week. He had the house, buildings, gardens and orchard, rent, tithes and levy, free, and £5 to find coal for the use of the House and Vestry Room, £1 for brushes, ropes, brooms etc. On quitting, three months' notice was to be given on either side.

In 1832 the Overseers looked into the question of removing the paupers to the Lunatic Asylums at Gloucester and Stafford, but this plan fell through because later in the year there was a cholera epidemic in Worcester and the county.

In June the following year the Vestry reported that they had purchased the shares of two of the shareholders who had invested in the late workhouse at Fearnall Heath for £20 each to be paid out of the next poor rate levy. The Vestry agreed to pay the remaining shareholders 4% interest per annum. They also agreed to again take possession of the old workhouse at Fearnall Heath, lay down rules and employ a proper person.

The Vestry had every intention of purchasing the old workhouse at Fearnall Heath from William Wall at a cost of £525 raising the sum by loan on security of the Poor Rate but on the advice of the parish solicitor rented the property instead at £26.5s.0d per annum.

In March 1833 George Thompson and his wife were appointed superintendents of the workhouse at a salary of £60 per annum plus coals and candles on condition that their time would be wholly devoted to the affairs of the parish. The parishes of Warndon, Martin Hussingtree, Crowle and Hindlip were again invited to send their parish poor to the Fearnall Heath Workhouse at an annual cost of £6, and Salwarpe, Himbleton and Tibberton at £7. The scale of charges was 4s.0d per week for those above 7 years old and 3s.0d per week for those under 7 years old.

The parishes had to provide all bedding. Those who were capable of labour were put to cultivating the land surrounding the workhouse, repairing the parish roads or pounding hemp. The workhouse was a place of strict control over the paupers and those who were able-bodied though disinclined to work quit the house.

Harsher treatment was meted out to the poor. When entering the workhouse married couples had separate beds and children under 7 years of age slept in the same room with their parents, the boys with the men and the girls with the women. When John Blake and his family were ordered into the workhouse he was told that he was capable of working on the roads breaking stone and considered able to earn 9s.0d per week. If he refused to work the Governor would take him before the magistrates for punishment. A similar order applied to a John Cartwright who was expected to earn 8s.0d per week. A quantity of hemp was ordered to employ several paupers in beating it and the Overseers enquired at Worcester Gaol of the quantity that should be pounded in a day. An Elizabeth Everall was taken into the workhouse, properly clothed, and then kept to the beating of hemp. The Vestry allowed a local gravel pit owner to employ paupers at the rate of 6d per yard digging out gravel, the paupers providing the shovels and the owner providing the wheelbarrows.[5]

---

[5] *WRO. BA 2683/3.*

John Mathew Gutch, Overseer of the Poor for the year 1833, submitted a lengthy report the following year to the ratepayers of the conditions of the workhouse. During his term of office he had made a careful note of every pauper on the relief books and had informed them that no more money would be given towards the payments of cottage rents, and any able-bodied persons who applied for relief and were dissatisfied with the allowance could find asylum in the workhouse where employment would be given to them and would be maintained according to a scale of diet approved by two magistrates – a diet so ample and good that no complaint had been made by any pauper in the workhouse. As if they had dared to do so!

The Poor Law Amendment Act 1834 put a stop to the practice of granting systematic out-door relief to able-bodied men who had learnt to depend on it. This Act empowered the building of workhouses controlled by 'Guardians of the Poor'. John Mathew Gutch went on in his report to state that in his opinion, a Board of Guardians could not possibly obtain the information of the concerns of a parish, the characters and wants of the poor.

The Vestry resolved that after the death of any pauper the Assistant Overseer was to enquire into the circumstances of the children of the deceased as to whether they could pay for the funeral so that he did not have to pay for the deceased's funeral at the expense of the parish.

The rent being paid for the workhouse was insufficient to keep down the interest of the money expended and the trustee and shareholders put the premises up for auction. Benjamin Lucy of Fearnall Heath purchased the property for a very low figure that did not cover the full amount owing to them, and set up a shoemaker's business in the former workhouse but died soon afterwards. His widow Ann and son, William, took over the business. She later married John Ely, another shoemaker, who was also the licensee of the 'Plough Inn', later the 'Live and Let Live' near to the old workhouse. The Blake family, former inmates of the workhouse, lived in a small cottage behind the old workhouse.

In 1844 Ann Lucy applied to the Church Building Commissioners to sell a portion of the land formerly occupied by the old workhouse for a new chapel but was refused permission on the grounds that the Vestry might possibly attempt to claim some interest in the property. However, the Vestry resolved that they had never had any interest in the workhouse beyond that of renting it from the parties who had contributed to its erection and therefore they had no legal claim to any right of title.

The Droitwich Union Workhouse was completed in May 1838 at a cost of £5,500 with accommodation for 130 paupers. Twenty-six parishes including Claines became part of the Union that sent their paupers to Droitwich. By then Worcester city boundary had extended to Barbourne Brook and the Vestry passed a resolution that the county part of Claines should no longer contribute to the City's poor levy.[6]

Dissatisfaction at the rates of wages paid to agricultural workers had intermittently broken out since 1834 and in 1872 great agitation spread to several Worcestershire villages including Fearnall Heath, and in that year The Oddfellows Lodge was started in the village to establish a fund to give assistance to men out of work, in old age, sickness and death. Meetings were held at the 'White Hart' public house once a fortnight.

In 1888 Mrs. Susannah Jolley of Tapenhall House died and left several charitable bequests that came into effect after the death of her daughter in 1928. She left £1,600 of railway stock of which one quarter was given to the Priest of the Roman Catholic Church in Sansome Place, Worcester, towards church maintenance and services. The remaining three quarters to the Charity Commissioners for England and Wales to apprentice poor children in the parish to useful trades as approved by them. £4 to be paid on Christmas Day in equal shares between four widows, £4 for four poor old men and £8 for coal for poor people in the same parish. 'The Parish' excluded the several ecclesiastical districts taken out of Claines by 1888.

William Dobbs of Fernhill Heath died in 1898 and after several bequests left three cottages known as Rose Cottages in Fernhill Heath. The rents from the cottages were given in coals and warm clothing each winter to the needy and determining poor of Fernhill Heath to those residing between the third and fourth mile posts on the Droitwich Road.

The old workhouse was probably purchased by the 3rd Lord Hindlip and formed part of the Hindlip Estate. The house was divided up into three cottages, Nos. 1, 2 and 3 Fir Cottages. The Mytton family; Herbert, then his son, Jack, built a butcher's shop onto the side of No. 1 Fir Cottage. No. 3 Fir Cottage eventually became the district nurse's house. In 1963 Nos. 1 and 2 were sold as part of the Hindlip Estate sale. Later, the district nurse moved to a new house in Perrycroft Close.

---

[6] WRO. BA 2683/22.

In 1968 Staite Developments purchased the three cottages, which were then renovated and sold.

Chapter 7
Hindlip School

In 1869 Henry Allsopp built Hindlip School at Sandyway. The first pupils accepted were limited to his estate workers, but in 1870 education opportunities became freely available to all children. From its foundation the school came under the control of both the Local Education Board, later to become the Local Education Authority (LEA) and the Worcester Diocesan Education Board. Regular inspections were made by the Local Education Board to test the children on their ability in reading, writing and arithmetic, and the Diocesan Board tested on the Catechism and the Bible.

The school opened on Monday, 18th October 1869, and the first Headmaster was Mr. Joseph Davey. On that day 24 children were admitted and by the end of the first week the number had risen to 41 on the register. The school continued to attract new pupils and by the end of the first year the number averaged 63.

The children sat on forms in one main room and were at first taught by the Headmaster, the only teacher. Their education was basic, the three 'R's'; reading, writing and arithmetic, religious instruction and hymn singing. As time went on more subjects were introduced, map reading, geography, domestic economy and sewing. The first HM Inspector's report of 1871 stated that 'The school has made creditable progress during the 15 months it has been under Mr. Davey. The children passed a fair examination in Scripture, Reading and Spelling and acquitted themselves in Arithmetic and Needlework. More attention should be paid to Catechism, and in copy-setting care should be taken to give exercises that are well graduated according to the age of the children and the time they have been in school.'

By 1872 the number of pupils on the roll had increased to 100 and pupil teachers were employed. Pupil teachers were elder children who had attained good marks in school subjects and were entrusted to teach groups of younger pupils. In 1876 an Education Act was passed establishing the right that all children should receive elementary education and the 1880 Education Act required attendance at school between the ages of 5 and 10 at which age a child could leave school. By the turn of the 20th century the school leaving age had been raised to 12 years.

School holidays were fixed at 2 weeks for Easter, 1 week at Whitsun, 4 weeks Harvest Holiday in August and 2 weeks at Christmas. Absenteeism was a problem, helping at home and in the fields were more important and after the Harvest Holidays some of the children did not return to school immediately as they were engaged in gleaning in the harvest fields where they could earn 6d a day. On one occasion in 1872 the children went to Worcester Races instead of attending school! Frequent illnesses of mumps, measles, chickenpox and influenza, kept children at home, and the more serious illnesses of scarlet fever and diphtheria, which were notifiable diseases, closed the school for several weeks.

The school numbers continued to grow and following the Local Education Board Inspector's report in 1880 the schoolroom was enlarged. Pupil teachers continued to assist the Headmaster and in 1885 the first appointment of an assistant mistress was made.

At that time the school inspector usually went on horseback to Claines School first and depending on what he said to the Headmaster the school's best runner would be despatched to either Hindlip or Salwarpe School to warn of his impending approach!

The school also doubled up as somewhere to hold evening entertainment and concerts were regularly held that included songs, glees, piano solos and recitations given by the villagers.

On the 3rd April 1887 Lord Hindlip died. For nearly 20 years he had financially supported the school and treated the children to Christmas tea with magic lantern shows and other tea treats at Hindlip Hall. The 2nd Lord Hindlip continued with the tradition of school treats. On the occasion of Queen Victoria's Golden Jubilee in 1897 the schoolchildren and Sunday schoolchildren were entertained to tea at Court Farm, Hindlip, and were presented with Jubilee mugs, medals and buns.

The accounts for the year 1892 show that the income for the school was derived from a Government Grant of 17s.0d per head and a Fee Grant of 10s.0d per head. Mr. J. A. Wheeler, the second Headmaster, and the Sewing Mistress received a joint salary of £140.0.0d per annum, presumably the Headmaster's wife taught too. There were two assistant teachers on a salary of £30 each per annum, and a Monitress at £2.12.0d per annum. For the year the school cleaning cost £4.0.0d, fuel £14.0.0d, stationery £6-£12 and repairs £5-£10.[1]

---

[1] WRO. BA 9875/11.

By 1893 there were 103 children in the main schoolroom and 45 infants in the smaller room, far too many for the school and the inadequate replacement lavatory block that had been built a few years earlier. Another year passed and the school buildings were inspected with a view to taking them down. The school was moved to the Mission Room in Fernhill Heath, as the building was no longer being used for worship.

The former Mission Room was adapted to make a large main room, two classrooms with cloakrooms and lobbies to accommodate 177 older children and 54 infants. On Monday, 1st October 1894, the new school opened with 130 pupils on the register. Evening concerts began again in the new school.

Absenteeism still remained a problem and to encourage regular attendance the school managers decided to award annual book prizes, later on prizes for scripture and good conduct were also awarded.

In January 1903 the Headmaster, Mr. J. A. Wheeler, was awarded a Diploma and Medal for 25 years' service and as a memento of the Coronation of King Edward VII from the Worcestershire County Council.

The appointment of a new Headmaster, Horace Teare, in 1908 brought further changes to the curriculum and gardening for the boys was introduced in 1910 with the 3rd Lord Hindlip providing a piece of ground

Fig 38. Hindlip School. c1902.

Fig 39. The Overseas Club. 1915

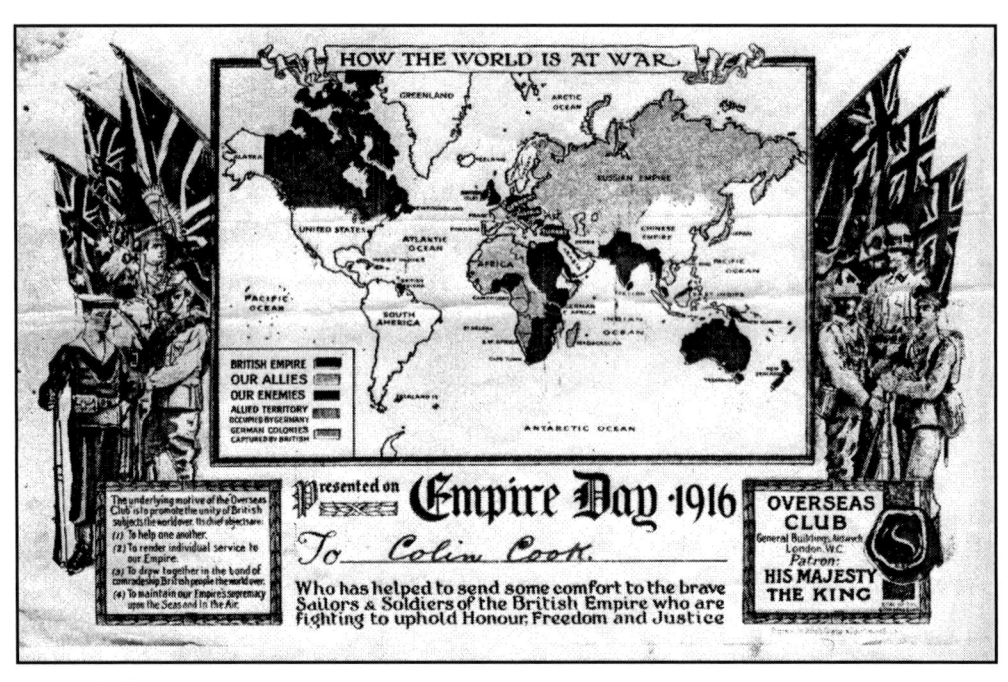

Fig 40. Empire Day. 1916

off Post Office Lane. At the outbreak of World War I cookery classes for the girls were held in Claines School.

In 1914 there were 203 pupils on the roll, by 1915 the number had reduced to 173, many children had left school because there was plenty of work.

Compulsory conscription into the War did not commence until May 1916 and the School Managers supported the Headmaster's appeal that he was needed to continue his work as a schoolmaster, but later that year he lost his appeal before the Droitwich Rural Tribunal and joined the RGA. During his absence two Deputy Headmasters were appointed, John Wooldridge in 1916 and Thomas Styles 1916-1918. Horace Teare was wounded in his hand and discharged from service and resumed his Headship in April 1918.

The school learnt in September of that year that a past pupil of the school, Pte. George Shepherd of the Canadian Regiment had been killed in action. The headmaster attended the funeral at Martin Hussingtree Church and the school sent a wreath.

During the war Mrs. Teare joined the teaching staff and as part of her war work she organised many sewing evenings at the school for the ladies in the village, the schoolgirls too made garments for the soldiers.

In September 1918 the Ministry of Food asked the school to help with blackberry picking, the fruit to be sent on for the army and navy. The children picked 14½ cwt of blackberries over 1½ days and for their efforts were paid £20.11.3d. (£20.62p).

With the introduction of the 1918 Education Act the school-leaving age rose to 14. Infants 5–7 years, Juniors 7–11 years and Seniors 11–14 years.

On the 1st June 1920 all the staff resigned in protest over a difference of opinion with the LEA with regard to salaries and the school was closed for two days.

In 1925 Mrs. Mildred Berkeley moved into Fernhill Heath House. She was a lady who was very interested in education and quickly became a regular and popular visitor to the school encouraging the children in their lessons, and presenting prizes for spelling, poetry, reading and needlework. Every pupil who left school was presented with a Bible given by her. On many occasions she entertained the school to tea and games in her garden.

The cookery lessons at Claines had continued throughout the war years and when the Memorial Hall was opened in 1922 the lessons were transferred there. One day in January 1929 the teacher who was taking the class rushed back into the school asking the Headmaster to come quickly as several girls had fainted. On investigation it was found that the gas boiler was leaking and the fumes could not escape. The school managers decided that the Memorial Hall was no longer suitable for cookery lessons and Mrs. Berkeley donated a hut in her grounds so that the lessons could continue. An unusual event in the 1920s was the Annual Feast of Plum Puddings in the month of December when the cookery class made five large Christmas puddings and 11 lbs of sweets for the poor boys of St. Paul's School in Worcester.

By 1929 the school was facing financial problems. Up until then the Lords of Hindlip had supported the school but the 3rd Lord Hindlip had moved away to Derbyshire and felt disinclined to continue with the present arrangement of keeping the school in good repair, the cost of any structural alterations having been borne by him. The residents of neither Hindlip nor Martin Hussingtree ecclesiastical parishes had ever been called upon to financially assist towards the upkeep of the building. There was a nominal rent of one shilling but this had never been asked for and never been paid. This arrangement was entered into to safeguard Lord Hindlip's property rights. Lord Hindlip wished the school to be retained by the School Managers as a Church School with the same conditions and tenancy so long as the Managers would keep the building in repair.

A public meeting was held in June 1929 at which it was resolved to retain the school as a Church School and Mr. Harry Tyler of Martin Hall Farm, Martin Hussingtree, on behalf of the school managers guaranteed the annual sum that was necessary to maintain the building.

The children were encouraged to help other children less fortunate than themselves and for many years the school supported the Waifs and Strays Society, (later known as The Church of England Children's Society) at the Paul Amphlett Boys' Home, an orphanage at Witton, Droitwich, by contributing towards the upkeep of the 'Hindlip School Cot'.

War was declared on the 3rd September 1939 and the Headmaster, Horace Teare, had already been recalled from his holidays a few days earlier. He was instructed not to open the school until the LEA gave the order. The school re-opened on the 11th September and 69 children from

Birmingham Rookery Road CS Junior, Handsworth, Birmingham, were admitted. The children were billeted amongst the neighbourhood, three teachers with Mrs. Berkeley at Fernhill Heath House and two teachers with Col. Chichester at The Grange, Claines. The school operated in two shifts from 9 am to 12.30pm or 1 pm for their own children, and from 1 pm to 4.30 pm or 5 pm for the evacuees. At the beginning of October HM Inspector for Schools was called in with a view to the evacuees using the Memorial Hall for lessons. However, by the middle of October all the evacuees had returned home. The following year nine evacuees were in school having been sent to the area from Birmingham and London, they were all living with relations in the area.

In June 1940 a number of children from Clacton-on-Sea were billeted in the village. As there were not enough places for them in the school it was decided they should be taught in the Memorial Hall.

The children had received gas masks as early as April 1939 and in 1940 they took part in air-raid evacuation tests. The first daylight "Alert" warning sounded in the middle of a school afternoon in February 1941, the children went to their safety stations, the alert lasted for 20 minutes when the "All Clear" was sounded.

Concerts were held at the school in aid of the Red Cross Fund. The school became a selling centre for the Droitwich & District War Weapons Week, 17th-24th May 1941, and during that time over £8,500 was raised.

On the 23rd May 1944 Miss Wynne, a teacher at the school for 52 years of unbroken service retired. She had taught Highest Junior Class for 37 years. She was presented with a cheque for 26 guineas. On the same day Mrs. Mildred Berkeley was buried at her old home, Cotheridge. A memorial service for Mrs. Berkeley was held at Martin Hussingtree Church on the 25th May.

Mr. Teare, the Headmaster was due to retire in August 1945 but the LEA requested him to continue pending the future state of the school. Sadly his wife died in November 1945 having taught at the school for 30 years. Mr. Teare retired at the end of March 1946 having served almost 38 years.

The next Headmaster was Mr. Vernon Hedges who commenced in June 1946 and retired in March 1959.

Mr. Hedges introduced outings to local factories and farms for the older children about to start work. Woodwork classes for the boys commenced in Droitwich and domestic subjects for the girls began again. A school holiday camp was held at Hindlip in 1950 and afterwards the Malvern Project Scheme was introduced with children staying there for one week. Rural studies commenced at 'Oakfield House' in Fernhill Heath.

A report of the school in 1946 disclosed that there were 130 children aged between 5-14, 3 female teachers and one headmaster. Children came from Claines, Hindlip, Martin Hussingtree, Tibberton and Witton in Droitwich. The present site was deemed unsuitable. The school was only about 11 feet from the main road and the traffic noise was heard throughout the school. There was the possibility of a national motorway being constructed to take the traffic from Birmingham to Bristol that would bypass the village and reduce traffic noise and accidents. The school was in the centre of the community and no other site in the village would be more conveniently situated or likely to become available in the future. However, a year later the Development Plan proposals for Worcestershire LEA were published which included a new Hindlip school on a new site, yet to be found.

By this time too, the school had no income and was unable to carry out any repairs. The School Managers had no alternative but to apply to the Ministry of Education for the immediate grant of controlled status. The Hindlip Estate granted a lease to the LEA for 21 years at £100 per annum commencing in 1948.[2]

The 1944 Education Act introduced a selective secondary system of separate grammar, technical and modern schools and the school leaving age was raised to 15. Children at the age of 11 sat an examination for the Grammar School; those who failed or did not take the examination remained at the school. In 1950 the school became a Controlled School with five classes, ranging in years, 5-6, 6+-7+, 8+-9+, 10+-11+, 12+-15. In 1951 the school opened as a Primary School and all the senior children were transferred to St. Peter's CE School in Droitwich, with their Assistant Master, Mr. F. M. Hirons.

There was no provision for a new primary school in Droitwich and the children from the Witton area were admitted to Hindlip, by 1954 there were 198 children on the school register.

In 1951 the pedestrian crossing outside the school was removed because a new policy had been introduced claiming that it was better to

---

[2] WRO. BA 9954/31.

provide adult patrols and a local policeman saw the children safely over the road.[3] Later 'lollipop ladies' took over the job.

In July 1952 Miss Barton, a teacher for 44 years resigned.

In September 1955 a new secondary modern school at Witton, Droitwich, opened for children from the age of 11 years. Mr. Hedges retired in 1959 and was succeeded by Mr. Portman until 1962, followed by Mr. Hawkes until July 1978.

In 1970 the Chairman of the Diocesan Education Committee presented a scroll to the school from the National Society to commemorate 100 years of the founding of the school.

Fig 41. Hindlip School. 1956.

In September 1971 the school was constituted as a 5-9 First School. The changeover brought a radical reduction in numbers with 122 on the school roll and the teaching staff reduced to 4 members.

Mr. Hawkes introduced a number of changes with parents' evenings and

---

[3] *WRO. BA 10533/1.*

occasional educational school visits to places of interest. In 1971 the Parents' Teachers' Association was formed. The PTA held many social events that brought in much needed money to help with the purchase of schoolbooks and equipment.

The new appointment in 1978 of the next Head Teacher, Mrs. Gillian Welford, coincided with drastic cutbacks in education. The PTA was constantly fund raising to pay for basic essentials. An opportunity arose and was taken up in 1979 to rent the garden behind the Hairdressers shop next door as a grassed area with an entrance into the playground.

In 1980 the PTA dissolved and the Friends Association formed. The new Association had a more 'hands on' approach and began to meet parents with children entering the school and acquainting them with the formal running of the school.

For several years the school had held an annual Harvest Festival service and afterwards the children took harvest gifts to the elderly and sick in the village. This was discontinued and the harvest was then given to the WRVS who came into school and explained how their gifts would be used. Later the harvest gifts were passed to St. Paul's Hostel for the Homeless in Worcester.

Early in 1984 Hereford & Worcester County Council put forward a proposal of a joint partnership with North Claines Parish Council to provide a new school, replacing the existing Hindlip School, with an adjoining parish room, on 'The Brum' playing fields at an estimated cost of £130,000, with the cost shared between the County Council and the Parish Council, possibly opening in September 1987. An open meeting was held in the school to discuss the proposal which was unanimously thrown out by those present on the grounds that the costs could be borne by an increase in the rates, the new school was away from the centre of the village, and that there was a public footpath running alongside 'The Brum' that could attract undesirables.

The proposed school was not built and in 1989 the old building was upgraded with two classrooms turned into a hall that doubled up as a gymnasium, and an extension built on at the back that included a new classroom, a new cloakroom and lavatories.

Figs 42 & 43. New extension. 1989.

Chapter 8
From Rose Bank to Sandyway

Many properties in Fernhill Heath have an interesting history. From the 19th century onwards it became fashionable for home-owners in the village to name their houses and cottages and some were named after trees, shrubs and flowers; rose being the most popular. Properties were also named after the location, i.e. Dilmore House, Dilmore Cottage and Heath House.

Following is a miscellany of properties with some photographs, sale notices and advertisements.

Starting from the civil parish boundary at Rose Bank-

Oakfield House (The River School) and Lodge

Oakfield was once part of Puckpit Farm (The Grange), Claines, an estate of both copyhold and freehold land. In 1770 part of the freehold was sold to James Oliver who may have built Oakfield House on the former toot-hill. His son, another James, inherited in 1790 and following his death the estate passed in trust to his two sisters, Mary Oliver and Elizabeth Mason and afterwards to Elizabeth's husband, William Mason, and then to their son, Philip, who died in 1826. In his will, this estate, together with other properties, was to be sold and the proceeds divided up between his four brothers and one sister. However, his brother, Oliver, took Oakfield. In 1834 the house was leased at £180 per annum for 21 years to Mrs. Mary Marmont, the principal of the Oakfield Academy.

In 1841[1] there were 26 boarders ranging in age from 6 years to 15 years, with five teachers and 7 servants occupying the house. By 1851[2] the number of pupils had increased to 35 boarders aged between 12 years and 18 years who came from Lancashire, Cheshire, Gloucestershire, Staffordshire, and from as far away as Dublin, Nova Scotia, and India.

Mrs. Marmont came to the attention of the Claines Churchwardens because she had not paid for the seat she occupied under the Belfry. Then there were 220 free sittings and 300 paid seats. The Churchwardens ordered that she should be asked for 10 guineas to cover the 10 years she had used the Belfry.

---

[1] *1841 Census.*
[2] *1851 Census.*

Distinguished FREEHOLD MANSION, famed as "OAKFIELDS," crowning the summit of a commanding Eminence, in the midst of its own Grounds, a Site of incomparable beauty, only 2½ miles from the City of Worcester.

TO BE SOLD BY AUCTION,
BY HOBBS & SON,

At the Star Hotel, Worcester, on Wednesday, the 29th day of August, 1855, at five o'clock;

A SPACIOUS FREEHOLD MANSION HOUSE, of great Architectural merit, with PLANTATIONS and GROUNDS, called

"OAKFIELDS,"

having every accommodation for a FAMILY of IMPORTANCE; and near

THIRTEEN ACRES OF CAPITAL LAND,

in the Parish of CLAINES, two and a half miles from the City of Worcester, and *near a Railway Station.*

THIS ELEGANT & ATTRACTIVE MANSION

has been built but a few years, in the most substantial manner, at a very considerable but judicious outlay and completed throughout regardless of expense, yet with every consideration to convenience, which it *now possesses in a remarkable degree.* It is in perfect repair, and happily erected on an

EMINENCE NOT TO BE EQUALLED

in this county, commanding Views over the rich and fertile District of WORCESTER, HEREFORD, and GLOUCESTER of

IMMENSE EXTENT AND ALMOST MATCHLESS BEAUTY,

amongst which the

NOBLE HILLS OF MALVERN ARE A DISTINGUISHED FEATURE,

and the Country immediately around, gradually

SLOPING AND ADORNED WITH STATELY TREES,

has a most PARK-LIKE APPEARANCE, whilst at an agreeable distance the

VENERABLE CATHEDRAL AND GRACEFUL SPIRES OF WORCESTER,

towering over the MASS of SURROUNDING WOOD COMPLETE THE FASCINATION OF THE SCENE.

The approach from the Turnpike-road is by a

CARRIAGE DRIVE WINDING THROUGH THRIVING PLANTATIONS

to a FLIGHT of STONE STEPS and *Paved Promenade* with VERANDA over leading to an ENTRANCE HALL.

TWO HANDSOME SUITES OF LOFTY ROOMS,

communicating by Folding Doors; Staircase, Lofty well proportioned Drawing-room, with Ante-room, and Breakfast-room; also a Secondary Staircase, and

FIFTEEN BED-ROOMS,

Dressing-rooms, Kitchens, Pantries, and necessary Offices; Stable, Double Coach-house, &c. &c. A good KITCHEN GARDEN, partly Walled, and Planted with Choice Fruit Trees.

A CONSERVATORY

and tasteful FLOWER GARDEN.

No.	Names of Pieces.	State.	Quantity.
			A. R. P.
20	House, Buildings, Gardens, Yards, Paddock, Plantations, and Carriage Drive	....	2 3 19
21	Homestead	Pasture	2 3 31
22	Front Hill	Ditto	1 1 16
23	Footen Hill	Ditto	3 3 30
24	Jasper's Acre	Ditto	1 2 11
		Total	12 2 27

For further particulars apply to Mr. John Bolton, Solicitor, Dudley; Messrs. Hydes and Tymbs, Solicitors; Mr. John Jones, Solicitor; Messrs. Webb and Buck, Land Agents; and the Auctioneers, all of Worcester.

Fig 44. Sale of Oakfield. 1855.

Mrs Marmont died at Bellsize Park in London in 1877 aged 77 years and was buried at Claines in the same grave as Annabel Shepherd who may have been her daughter.

Oakfield House was sold in 1855 and the advertisement described it as 'A spacious freehold mansion house of great architectural merit with plantations and grounds of 13 acres.'

Henry Pidcock, a Worcester solicitor, purchased the house. After his death in 1862 the house was sold and purchased by Henry Carden an eminent Worcester surgeon, whose hobbies were flowers and art, particularly, the work of the Worcester artist, Benjamin Williams Leader. Henry Carden died in 1873 and his wife in 1879 and both were buried at Claines.

Oakfield House was again a school for Young Ladies in 1892 with the purchase of the property by William Davidson, a solicitor. His daughter was the school principal. During the Davidson's residency the pine trees in Claines Lane were planted so that the young ladies would not see the men going in and out of the Raven Inn on the Droitwich Road below the school!

In 1909 The Revd Joseph Bowstead Wilson and his wife, Catherine, retired to Oakfield. He died in 1911 and was buried at Knightwick. In memory of her husband his widow gave an organ and generator to Claines Church. Catherine Wilson continued to live at Oakfield until her death in 1939.

Just before the outbreak of World War II the house was requisitioned as a possible use either for the House of Lords or for soldiers to be billeted there. The government did not use the house and for the first two years of the War the Royal Artillery was there, followed by the Women's Land Army.

The house was sold in 1950 to the Worcestershire County Council and became a teachers' training centre specialising in horticulture. Later the gardens and greenhouses were used to supply plants for school gardens and Worcester city parks. The Schools Meals Service occupied part of the house and Claines schoolchildren walked to Oakfield for their school dinners.

There was some short-lived excitement during February 1961 when a heavy lorry making a delivery to Oakfield sank into the forecourt. Workmen discovered a brick-built tunnel varying in diameter between 3

Fig 45. Women's Land Army at Oakfield House.

feet and 6 feet and running some 50 yards from a wing of the building. Its purpose was not properly established although there were suggestions that it may have been an old sewer or an air inlet in the central heating system.[3]

In 1983 the training centre closed and the BBC wanted to make a film about the proposed closure but Hereford & Worcestershire County Council refused them permission. Worcester City Parks department had campaigned to save the 30-year-old garden from destruction. The department was moved to Pershore College of Horticulture, the County Council claiming that the move would save £30,000 per year.

In 1984 Oakfield House was put up for auction and sold to a development company but they were unable to get planning permission for their scheme. The lower bid put in by the Worcester Christian Trust enabled them to purchase the property and establish The River School that opened in 1985. The school is Christian, and takes both boys and girls, but it is not exclusive to any particular group or any one denomination, and does not exclude the less able or disadvantaged child.

Oakfield Lodge was built in 1860 with a gated entrance to the carriageway leading up to the house.

Morton House

This estate too, was once part of Puck Pit (The Grange), Claines. In 1853 just over 9 acres of land was sold for £1,200 to William Barneby, a Worcester solicitor. He also purchased a small piece of land from the Partridge sisters who owned the blacksmith's shop next door. William Barneby built a house called South Villa. Some time later it was either renamed Morton House, or it may have been his son, Thomas, a keen astronomer and a member of the FRAS, who built another new house with an observatory calling it, Morton House. In 1876 Thomas Barneby purchased 20 acres of land adjoining and opposite Morton House and several other plots of land on the east side of the Droitwich Road near to the railway from the Perdiswell estate. He died in 1894 and afterwards another solicitor, William Price Hughes lived there until his death in 1905.

Mrs. M. L. Ashton purchased the property. Two years before her death in 1928, a piece of land north of the grounds on the Droitwich Road was sold and the builders, Spicers Ltd., built Springfield House for George Foss, a Worcester seed merchant.

---

[3] *Worcester Evening News & Times. 13th February 1961.*

Fig 46. Oakfield Lodge. 1952.

WORCESTERSHIRE.

2½ miles from Worcester, 3½ from Droitwich,
23½ from Birmingham.

Morton House Estate

FERNHILL HEATH

To be sold by Auction on

MONDAY, SEPTEMBER 29th, 1930.

SOLICITORS:	AUCTIONEERS:
Messrs. Witham, Roskell, Munster & Weld,	Messrs. Geo. Yeates & Sons, F.A.I.,
1 Grays Inn Square,	8 Foregate Street,
London, W.C.1.	Worcester.

Fig 47. Morton House Estate Sale. 1930.

Mrs. Ashton died in 1930 and the County Police purchased Morton House. Just before the outbreak of World War II the house was requisitioned for the Ministry of Defence. The County Police were relocated to Worcester and after the War moved to their present headquarters at Hindlip Hall.

In 1950 Morton House was converted into the Civil Defence Headquarters. New stores were added on to the garage block behind the house in 1963 to serve as a general headquarters store during the 'Cold War' period. In 1968[4] the Civil Defence moved out and the offices of the Weights and Measures from Stourport and Upton-on-Severn moved in the following year.[5] In 1985 Morton House was sold and converted to a Rest Home for the elderly and is now both a Nursing and Rest Home.

Saturday, 25th June 1988 was a very special day for one of the residents, Miss Julia Holden, formerly of Station Road, who celebrated her 100th birthday with a bumper party for over 100 guests. In 1993 she had an even more spectacular celebration for her 105th birthday by jetting off for a day trip to Scotland in a Boeing 737.

The Blacksmith's Shop

In 1797 the copyhold blacksmith's shop and house was built and occupied by John Partridge.[6] He and his wife, Hannah, had one son, John, and two daughters, Sarah and Elizabeth. John Snr died in 1841 and his son in 1845. The blacksmith's shop was rented out and the two daughters remained in the house. Sarah later married James Cooper Cooke, a builder, and it seems likely that he divided the house into two properties. James and Sarah living in Dilmore Cottage and Elizabeth living in Elm Cottage. James died first and then Sarah in 1881 leaving all her personal property, Dilmore Cottage and her share in Elm Cottage to her sister, Elizabeth, and afterwards to their niece Sarah Cayzer.

Elizabeth moved into Dilmore Cottage and rented out Elm Cottage. She died in 1896 aged 90. In her will she set out precise details of a wooden fence dividing the gardens of the two cottages with a frontage of 26 yards abutting the public highway, and left them to Sarah Cayzer and afterwards to Sarah's son, Henry Plummer Cayzer when he attained the age of 21 years.

---

[4] *WRO. BA 461/30.*
[5] *WRO. BA 461/1.*
[6] *WRO. BA 5410/17 (ii).*

Both sisters included in their wills bequests to several married nieces on the understanding that they would receive 'the legacies to married women for their separate use and benefit.' This was a direct reference to the Married Women's Property Acts; the 1870 Act allowed women to retain £200 of their own earnings; the 1882 Act allowed women to own and administer their own property; the 1884 Act making a woman no longer a 'chattel' but an independent and separate person.

On the death of her aunt, Sarah Cayzer moved into the property next door, Dilmore House, until she died in 1901. Dilmore Cottage and Elm Cottage were rented out and later demolished, date unknown.

Dilmore Lane Junction (North), Site of Dilmore Lodge/Heddon House

In 1751 John Jew held 1 rood of copyhold land on which stood a cottage and garden paying 1s.0d per year to the Bishop of Worcester. The property changed hands in 1791 when William Hooper, a hop merchant, of St. Helen's Worcester, took over the lease until 1829 followed by John Downes. The cottage was later demolished. The land had more than doubled in size to 2 roods and 8 perches when James Sayer of Worcester built a new house in 1840 and Joseph Williams was his tenant, followed by William Finch, a solicitor, in 1843. In 1849 the property was known as Dilmore House with a garden, stabling, buildings and a coach house. Richard Baylis who lived in the house at that time purchased the copyhold lease from the Bishop of Worcester for £228.

Richard Baylis died in 1880 his wife having predeceased him in 1876 and his son in 1878 and the property, by then called Dilmore Lodge, was left to his two nephews who sold it to Thomas Buckle Pinkett of The Bell Hotel, Broad Street, Worcester, Hotel Keeper, for £800.[7] He died two years later and the house passed to his wife, Elizabeth, for life and afterwards to his three children. She died in 1895 and her will makes interesting reading for apart from other personal property she owned some very exquisite pieces of jewellery and each one was described in detail for the lucky recipients. In a codicil to her will she left her stepson, Frederick Pinkett, a valuable Flight & Barr Worcester jug.

---

[7] WRO. BA 2193/73 (iii).

Fig 48. Dilmore Lodge. c1900.

Dilmore Lodge was sold to William Prosser for £1,040 who shortly afterwards died in 1898 and his widow remained at Dilmore Lodge until her death.

Sometime after her death its new unknown owners changed the house name to Thorneycroft. Mr. Burcher then purchased the property and renamed it Heddon House. He lived there for some years before moving out. The house was not sold and eventually fell into a bad state of disrepair and was demolished in 1978 and the outbuildings in 1979. Over the years the land has become a derelict site.

Pear Tree House

In 1775 a copyhold cottage and garden measuring 82 yards by 19 yards was built on this site, the rent was 2s.0d per year payable to the Bishop of Worcester. Richard Lightband, a yeoman, leased the cottage. Another lease in 1807 describes the cottage as being leased by a William Potter of Edvin Loach with Richard Lightband the younger occupying the cottage. By 1833 he had fallen on hard times for a note in the Claines Manor Rental Books discloses that he could not pay a fine of £15.10.0d to the lord of the manor on account of his poverty. Mary Marmont of the Oakfield Academy paid the fine and took over the lease.[8] She let the cottage to a shoemaker called Tuffley who was employed by her to make all the shoes and dancing slippers for the young ladies at her Academy.

In 1837 the property was known as 'The Old House at Home', a beer and cider house, with a garden and a pear orchard behind. Thomas Hind was the publican for about 13 years.

In 1850 Henry White, a blacksmith, took over the cider house employing first W. A. Martin, then Benjamin Tuffley, another shoemaker.

The Mence family followed, John Mence, a retired farmer, and his two unmarried daughters. Pear Tree House was referred to in Henry White's will dated 1888 as, 'that dwellinghouse adjoining occupied by Miss Mence', which he left to his son, Joseph in 1899.

Fig 49. Pear Tree House. 1952.

---

[8] WRO. BA 5410/18 (viii).

It is not known when the house ceased trading but for many years a metal sign advertising 'The Old House at Home' hung on one of the exterior walls of the house. The pear trees growing up against the wall gradually hid the sign from view.

The Forge

When Henry White, a blacksmith, first moved into Fearnall Heath he rented the Partridge's blacksmith shop at the top of Red Hill, then later became the licensee of 'The Old House at Home'. Next door he built the house and forge in the early 1860s.

After his death the forge passed to his elder son, Joseph in 1899 and then to his younger son, Henry, in 1904. By 1908 Henry Haden had taken over the business and was the last blacksmith to occupy the forge. Towards the end of the 20th century the outbuildings were used as a cattery.

Fig 50. The Forge. 1952.

No. 214 and Tapenhall House (Formerly one property)

For several years during the 19th century the house was used as a retirement home for former tenants of Deans Green Farm (Danes Green Farm). Richard Franks and his wife occupied the house in 1820 and were followed by John and Susannah Worrall and their son, John. In 1844 the occupants were John Ross, a retired farmer, with his unmarried daughter, Margaret, and married daughter Susannah Jolley and her daughter, Annie. Susannah Jolley left a considerable amount of money to both the Roman Catholic Church in Worcester, and to Claines Church, of which the latter became known as the 'Susannah Jolley Charity'.

In 1935 Tapenhall House together with a 4-acre field at the rear of the property were sold by auction at the 'Bull Hotel', Fernhill Heath, for £820. The house and land were purchased by Mrs. Olive Miller of Rose Bank. The house was divided into two properties. In 1940 Mrs. Miller offered the land to the Parish Council for a recreation ground but World War II put this on hold and she withdrew her offer in 1952. Cresswell Close was later built on this land.

The Brum

The old name for this field was The Big Broom, a reference to the heathland shrub that once grew there. For many years the open space has been used as a recreation ground.

Goodwood

This Edwardian mansion was built around 1901 probably for John Turner who had won a considerable amount of money on an accumulator bet on the horses and named the house, Goodwood.

Heath House

The house was built around the late 1880s and first named Clifton Villa. Ernest Percy Thomas (Pumpy Thomas) lived there and was employed as an engineer in his father's business of manufacturing windmills and water pumps that were exported worldwide. In the late 1920s Pumpy Thomas moved across the road to 'Windyridge'. He also built the row of properties called 'Windmill Cottages' in Dilmore Lane, Claines. The 'Climax' Works where the windmills and pumps were made was in the Droitwich Road

WORCESTERSHIRE.

Particulars and Plan
OF A
FREEHOLD COUNTRY PROPERTY
KNOWN AS
TAPENHALL HOUSE,
FERNHILL HEATH,
WORCESTERSHIRE,

with Valuable Arable Field at the rear

about 4 acres.

To be Sold by Auction by

WILLIAM P. SEABRIGHT, F.A.I.

At the Bull Hotel, Fernhill Heath,
ON
WEDNESDAY, NOVEMBER 27th, 1935,
AT 7 O'CLOCK P.M. PUNCTUALLY.

Subject to Conditions to be produced at the time of Sale.

Further particulars may be obtained of :—Messrs. Manby & Steward, Solicitors, 14 Waterloo Road, Wolverhampton (Tel. 20337); Mr. John E. Seabright, a.r.i.b.a., Architect and Surveyor, 1, Corbett Avenue, Droitwich Spa (Tel. 66); or The Auctioneer, 5, Foregate Street, Worcester (Tel. 1408).

Phillips & Probert Ltd., Printers, Worcester.

Fig 51. Tapenhall House sale notice. 1935.

next door to the 'Perdiswell' public house and closed down in the 1960s after his death.

The house name was changed to Heath Side, and the next occupant appears to have been Miss Caroline Bough who took in genteel ladies of retirement age and provided them with a good home. Miss Bough owned the small paddock (The Haven bungalow) next to The Brum playing fields where she kept a pony. She was often seen around the village and surrounding area in her pony and trap. After her death in 1969 the house was sold and became a private house. It was sold again and converted into Heathside Hotel in 1983.

No. 2 Mayhill Cottages

The cottage is one of a pair of semi-detached cottages, built in 1883 for Emma Anthonies. The cottages were small, two rooms up and two down, they were first called Rose Cottages then later changed to Rose Cottage and Rose Villa. On the 1891 census Emma Anthonies lived in Rose Cottage and Rose Villa is described as the County Police Station and was occupied by Police Officer Alfred Hayes and his family.[9] His beat was in the village, Claines, Spellis, Hindlip, Martin Hussingtree, Ladywood and Salwarpe. By the turn of the 20th century the cottage was no longer police property.

The 'White Hart' Public House

Fig 52. Fernhill Heath Fete 1909. Outside the 'White Hart' public house. Licensee J. Bricknell.

---

[9] *1891 Census.*

Fig 53. Fernhill Heath and Hindlip Mothers' Meeting excursion in 1910. Location unknown

The old piggeries and slaughterhouse

This small tumbledown building is in the field next to Hurst Cottage (formerly Hurst Farmhouse) in Hurst Lane and is all that is left of the piggeries and slaughterhouse used by Hubert and Jack Mytton who had their butcher's shop adjoining the old workhouse in the village.

Fig 54. The old piggeries and slaughterhouse

The Village looking south

When this photograph was taken both public houses were calling themselves 'hotels' offering bed, breakfast and an evening meal.

Fig 55. L-R. Preston's Garage, 'White Hart Hotel', the railway cottage and 'Bull Hotel'. c. late 1930s.

Preston's Garage

In the 1920s a Mr. Preston began a cycle and motorcycle business in a tin hut on this site. Benjamin Law purchased the business and later his son-in-law, George Jeffrey, took over. A car showroom and garage replaced the tin hut and a large clock mounted in a prominent position on the exterior wall facing the Droitwich Road was a village landmark. Motorists used to check the time as they drove through the village. The petrol pumps were in front of the showroom and motorists ran their vehicles onto the side of the road to fill up. The car showroom and garage were demolished in 1988.

Fig 56. Preston's garage sold 18th July 1988

Bull Inn (formerly The Durham Ox)

Fig 57. Bull Inn (Southern aspect). No longer a hotel in 1954!

G. S. Baylis, Baker & Confectioner

Fig 58. Brenda Baylis outside her father's shop, G. S. Baylis, Baker & Confectioner

In 1895 George Hunt Baylis of Witton, Droitwich, purchased the property for his son, George Spencer Baylis, from the baker, Henry Phippen. The sale included a house, shop, bakehouse, stable, coach house, storeroom, cottage, piggeries, slaughterhouse and other buildings for £745. Within 10 years his son had established himself as a baker, grocer and trader in farm animal feeds. He supplied groceries to both the wholesale and retail trade in Claines, Worcester, St. Johns and the villages of Kempsey, Norton, Powick, and Temple Laugherne.

A local resident purchased the items in Fig 59 in early December 1905. The prices bear no relation to today's costs and some of the items are no longer sold. An agricultural worker's wage in 1905 was about 14s.0d per week.

During World War I George Baylis was the only baker in the area and employed 17 years old George Clinton as a baker's deliveryman.

Colin Cook who lived in Sling Lane was about 7 years old in 1917 and recalled a tale many years later of a day in one of the school holidays when he helped George with his round. Colin's parents' house was the last house on his round. Colin had recently acquired two Belgian hares

1½ lb Raisins	1½d.	½ lb Candles	2d.	Scones			3d.
1½ lb Sultanas	6d.	Blacking	1d.	Blue (Laundry)			½d.
1½ lb Currants	6d.	1 lb Corned Beef	6d.	Starch	"		1d.
1 lb Peel	5½d.	½ lb Salt Butter	6½d.	½ lb Soap "			1½d.
2 Nutmegs	1½d.	Wood	3d.	3 Powders			2d.
½ lb Bacon	4d.	1oz Tobacco	3d.	Small tin Mustard			1d.
¼ lb Tea	5d.	Matches	½d.	Bicarbonate of Soda			1d.
2 lb Sugar	5d.	Tin Nestles	3d.	2 Vinegars			3d.
½ lb Cheese	4d.	1 Pkt Frys Cocoa	2d.	2 ozs Spice			1½d.
Bread	5½d.	Sweets	1d.	Rabbit			11d.
½ lb Butter	7d.	Tin of Salmon	7d.	Biscuits			7d.
Parisian Essence	10½d.	Marmalade	3½d.				

Fig 59. Grocery prices in December 1905.

but he was finding it difficult to keep them in food as by then food rationing was in force so he devised a plan to get some for free.

He had noticed that there were small piles of crumbs on the scrubbed wooden shelves and bigger flakes on the floor of the white hooded delivery cart. He asked George if rabbits would eat breadcrumbs, George said "Yes, and would you like them". He swept the crumbs into a paper bag and after thanking him Colin made his way to the hutches in the garden. The hares only ate the larger flakes and were not interested in the crumbs! On the Monday morning he went out to play and caught up with George just after he had left the bakery. George helped him aboard and in no time at all Colin was tossing out the correct loaf on request that George caught and delivered. Whilst he was delivering Colin was busy inspecting every loaf and carefully 'trimming' any protruding flake and placing it in his bag leaving a very tidy loaf. The physical work and the mental concentration tired him and he was also getting very hungry working away with the smell of warm new bread. There was one batch loaf that did not look quite right and he stripped off the offending flakes at each side and this helped to quell his hunger but did not cure the obvious lack of shape. Gradually the loaf lost its original mould and it seemed to be getting a tunnel through its middle end, by then Colin didn't have the heart to pass it over to George for delivery. As they arrived at the last place for delivery – Colin's home, George called out "Two for your

Fig 60. George Baylis with his white hooded delivery carts.

Fig 61. George Baylis. The proud owner of a new delivery van.
Photograph taken near Rosedene in Sling Lane.

mother", and Colin passed him the last two loaves hoping that he would not notice the 'damaged goods'. He appeared not to, but he heard his mother say, "What is wrong with this loaf, George?" Peeping over the tailboard of the cart, he saw George point to him and utter one solitary word 'MICE'. He knew then that the game was up!

Sometime after World War II the shop was altered with the grocery and bakery trading from the room on the left-hand side and a branch of the Midland Bank used the room on the right-hand side, opening part-time for several years. After the Bank closed an antique dealer took over the shop.

The bakery business was wound down and after the grocery shop ceased trading that, too, became an antique business, the new owner having acquired the smaller shop next door.

Edgar Davis Antiques
THE OLD BAKERY
FERNHILL HEATH
WORCESTER

Fine Furniture & Works Of Art
19th and 20th Century
Watercolours and Oils

*Georgian, Victorian, Edwardian
Furniture and Effects*

Worcester, Doulton and Wedgewood
Porcelain

Gold and Silver Jewellery

Open Monday-Tuesday-Wednesday 9-6pm
Friday-Saturday 9-6pm
Sunday 10-4pm

We wish to purchase any of the above items for cash
TELEPHONE: (0905) 51787

Fig 62. Edgar Davis Antiques. 1985.

High Barn (Formerly The Laurels)

The house was built between 1842-3 by Henry Bradley Morris. An entry in the Claines Manor Rent Books states that a cottage and garden standing on 38 perches was an 'encroachment on Vernal Heath'. Soon after the house was built the left hand downstairs front room was turned into a shop. Work on the new railway track was in progress and money was to be made from the navvies.

Fig 63. High Barn (Formerly The Laurels).

By 1851 Henry Morris and his family had moved to Birmingham. The Revd Arthur Gough leased the house for a short time as a boys' boarding school. Henry Morris died in 1852 and the house was left to his eldest son who sold it to his sister, Susannah Ann Morris for £60. Three years later she married Edwin Timms but they did not live there and the house was sold in 1866 to William Copple for £350.

William Copple died in 1878 leaving an estate of under £100 including the house to his wife, Mary. She died in 1910 and left bequests amounting to £5,250. The house and residue of her estate passed to her great niece,

> *Desirable detached* FREEHOLD COTTAGE RESI-
> DENCE *with productive* GARDEN *and* TENEMENT
> *in the rear, situate at*
> ## FEARNALL HEATH,
> *in the Parish of* CLAINES, *in the County of Worcester*
> ## TO BE SOLD BY AUCTION,
> ### BY MR. NATHANIEL TAYLOR,
> At the Bull Inn, Fearnall Heath, near Worcester, on Thursday, 5th day of July, 1866, at five o'clock in the afternoon, subject to conditions to be then produced;
>
> THAT most desirable and compact FREEHOLD COTTAGE RESIDENCE, pleasantly situate in the Village of FEARNALL HEATH aforesaid, and now in the occupation of Mr. Mee, with productive GARDEN planted with choice FRUIT TREES. The House, which is replete with every comfort and convenience for a genteel family, contains a private Entrance-hall, two front Sitting-rooms, Kitchen, Back Kitchen, Pantry, four Bed-rooms, large Attic, Closet, underground Cellar, Pump of excellent Water, and other conveniences.
>
> Also that comfortable TENEMENT with GARDEN in the rear.
>
> The situation is undeniable, being so contiguous to the Railway Station, adjoining a good road, and within three miles of the City of Worcester. To the small Capitalist it offers a safe and improving Investment, and for occupation it is most desirable. A portion of the Land having a considerable Frontage to the Road, is adapted for Building purposes.
>
> To view apply to the Tenants, and for further particulars to Mr. Nathaniel Taylor, Shaw-street, Worcester.

Fig 64. Sale notice. The Laurels. 1866.

Ivy Lane

Mary Catherine Bell Holmes who died the following year and her husband inherited the property. The Holmes family lived in the house until 1950.

Behind The Laurels in Ivy Lane was Deal Cottage, now The Byre, where a member of the Holmes family lived for many years.

Fig 65. Byre Cottage, Ivy Lane. c1970.

The Live and Let Live Public House

An amusing story was told in the Berrow's Worcester Journal, 6th September 1902, titled 'A Plum-stone Chase'. Five Worcester men were charged at Worcester Magistrates' Court for stealing between 30 and 40 lbs of Victoria plums the property of Sarah Henney, the licensee of the 'Live and Let Live Public House (now demolished).

The defendants went to Mrs. Henney's on a Saturday night and took lodgings, intending to have a day's fishing the following day. They arose about 5 am and got over the fence into the garden and took the plums. When Mrs. Henney came down she noticed a number of plum stones and, on going into the garden, saw that a quantity of plums had been stolen from the trees.

P. C. Hemming was sent for and traced the plum stones for nearly a mile to where the defendants were fishing.

They all pleaded guilty and were each fined 10s 0d (50p), plus 1s. 0d (5p) to cover the cost of the plums.[10] The question is did the police

Fig 66. The Live And Let Live.   Far right - Harry Farley.   Date unknown.

---

[10] *Worcester Evening News & Times. 6th February 1902.*

constable really trace the men by following the dropped plum stones or did Mrs. Henney tell him where the men had gone fishing?

Under the terms of Mr. Henney's will the 'Live and Let Live' was to be sold after his wife's death.

In the late 1930s the public house was pulled down and a new one erected on this site.[11]

Fig 67. The 'Live and Let Live' public house built in the late 1930s.

The Butchers, Butchers Opening and Butchers Walk

Soon after the workhouse opened in 1813 a copyhold house with an adjoining butcher's shop was built on the opposite side of the Wich Road (the plot is now occupied by Hillview Flats).

The butcher's shop closed in 1903 after the death of the last butcher, John Emuss.

Butchers Opening, later Butchers Walk, was extended when three cottages were built on the north side of the lane. The cottages replaced the copyhold cottage occupied by William Taylor in 1751.

The public footpath from Butchers Walk to the railway was at first an unofficial short cut that later became a permanent public footpath down to the station. The path linked up to two footpaths branching off Station Road, one going across to Danes Green and the other to Lower Town, the latter was closed in the 1930s.

---

[11] *Birmingham City Archives. MS161. B/9/6/2/3. Fols. 4669 & 4759.*

Staymore Café

The tearooms and gardens were a popular stopping-off point for cyclists who rode through the village and for many years a Cycling Touring Club sign hung on a tall post near the pavement. Later the premises catered for transport workers and doubled up as an afternoon venue for villagers who enjoyed a game of whist.

Next door to the tearooms was a semi-detached house, behind which was an attached grocery, hardware and newsagents business owned by Nellie Hope until her death in 1944. The business was sold and purchased by Mrs. Stezaker.

Fig 68. Staymore Café. 1954.

By direction of the Executors of the late Mrs. N. M. Hope.

PARTICULARS

OF

FREEHOLD

Country Grocery and Hardware Stores with Tea Gardens

and Goodwill of the Business;

MODERN VILLA and COTTAGE

AT

FERNHILL HEATH

(3 miles from Worcester)

WHICH WILL BE OFFERED BY AUCTION

(Subject to Conditions of Sale)

BY

HENRY COOMBS & SMITH

AT THE BULL HOTEL, FERNHILL HEATH

ON WEDNESDAY, 6th SEPTEMBER, 1944

At **6.0 p.m.** precisely.

Vendor's Solicitors - MESSRS. E. ROBERTS & SON, 8, Pierpoint Street, Worcester.
Auctioneers - - MESSRS. HENRY COOMBS & SMITH, 47, Foregate Street, Worcester.

Herald Printers (Worcester) Ltd., Exchange Street, Worcester.

Fig 69. Sale notice. 1944.

By direction of the Executors of the late Mrs. N. M. Hope.

PARTICULARS

LOT 1.—With Vacant Possession.

"The Tea Rooms"

FERNHILL HEATH

Comprising:—

A Well-built Freehold Semi-detached DWELLING HOUSE with GROCERY and HARDWARE STORES; OUTBUILDINGS and GARDEN.

The Premises comprise:—

Entrance Hall; Drawing Room with modern grate and oak mantelpiece, and bay window; Dining Room with modern grate and oak mantelpiece, and built-in fireproof safe; 4 Bedrooms.

Retail Shop with wide window and separate entrance, 2 Store Rooms behind, and Loft over.

Back Kitchen with long white procelain sink, and hot water supply tank; Pantry; Cellar; Wash-house; Privy; brick and tiled Coal House, and Store House; Cemented Yard, with soft water tank and semi-rotary pump; Well of good Water, with electric A.C. motor.

Open Cart Shed with slated roof, and Tool Shed; Wood and Galvanized Roof lean-to erection of Garage with double doors, with driveway entrance to Butchers Lane.

Wood Erection of Span-roof Tea Room with felt roof and wood floor, 19ft. 6in. by 14ft., and register grate; Annexe, comprising Cloak Room with double wash basins, and Lavatory with flushing tank; Verandah.

Gas and Electricity (power, heat and light).

Drainage to main sewer.

Telephone installed. Rateable Value, £18 10s. 0d.

The Garden is laid out with flower plots and lawns, and having concrete paths.

There is a good Frontage to the main road, with Car Park and two Entrances; also Frontage to Butchers Lane.

The above Property will be offered together with the GOODWILL of the Old-established Business of Tea Rooms, Grocery and Hardware Business and Newsagency.

VACANT POSSESSION will be given on completion of the purchase.

The Purchaser will be required to take to the Trade Fixtures and Fittings and Stock-in-Trade, at valuation.

This is an exceptional opportunity of acquiring an excellent Business and Premises.

The Property is situate on the main Worcester to Birmingham Road, and has been in the present hands about 25 years.

The Stores

A grocery and bakery business called the Central Stores opened in 1888 and at one time was also the village post office. In 1929 Charles Jackson owned the Central Stores. An insurance policy taken out by him on the premises for that year stated that the baker's oven was to be securely erected, no timber and kindling were to be placed over the oven, and excluded the cooking of Ship's Biscuits.[12] The biscuits were known as 'hard tack' and this gives an indication of how tough and tasteless they were.

Fig 70. The Stores. 1954.

In 1935 the business passed to his son, Albert and his wife who continued to run the shop and bakery business as 'The Stores' until they retired.

Local businesses in 1964.
Preston's Garage, S. C. Wilson, Van-Halen Hair Fashions, Fernhill Heath Post Office, F. Hadley, H. Mytton & Son and Dilmore Stores.

---

[12] *WRO. BA 10715/4.*

Fig 71. Local businesses and public houses in 1985.

Lilac Cottage between the Stores and the 'Half Way House'

Hubert Mytton's home. He kept the butcher's shop adjoining the old workhouse.

Fig 72. Lilac Cottage. 1954.

Fig 73. The 'Half Way House'. 1954.

The Drug Stores and Super Shop

The Drug Stores was a small black and white single storey building that stood on the corner of O'Keys Lane. Annie Hunt owned and served in the shop until her retirement. Frank Hadley, who had previously sold newspapers from a stand on the corner of Ivy Lane, took over the little shop to sell newspapers, confectionery and garden seeds. After he retired the shop passed through several hands until Peter Kasch purchased it. The building was demolished about 1984 and a new shop was built further back from the main road. In June 2000 the second building phase of the Super Shop opened.

Fig 74. Drug Stores. 1954.

Baptist Chapel

The Baptist Chapel opened in 1903. The secondhand wooden hut, Perry Hall, to the left of the photograph, was erected in 1953. One of the fund-raising events to raise money for the hall was a mile of pennies. In 1987 the old toilets and coalhouse block to the rear of Perry Hall were taken down and the Long Room together with new indoor toilets were built. Young offenders on community service helped with this project.

Fig 75. Fernhill Heath Baptist Chapel. 1954.

Since its opening the Baptist Chapel had been a branch chapel affiliated to Worcester Baptist Church in Sansome Walk, Worcester. In 1991 the Chapel became independent of Worcester and instated as a church – Fernhill Heath Baptist Church.

In the same year Perry Hall was taken down and transported to Romania for use as a church over there. The present hall was built on the Perry Hall site.

O'Keys Farm

In 1747 an Assessment for payment of the Poor Rate recorded that 'Harrison for Oakeys paid 2s.2d' to Claines Church. Charles Reynolds leased the copyhold farm in 1753. By 1806 the farm was owned by John Pearkes Lavender of Worcester. Lavender Road in Barbourne, Worcester, was named after him.

J. P. Lavender was for many years a partner in the bank of Farley, Lavender, Owen & Gutch, on The Cross, Worcester. The Gutch name became connected with the bank through John Mathew Gutch who married John Pearkes Lavender's daughter, Mary.

In 1834 John Gutch, as Overseer of the Poor of Claines, presented his lengthy and in parts a somewhat pompous report to the Claines ratepayers on the conditions of the Fearnall Heath Workhouse and his observations on the Poor Law Amendment Act 1834.

J. P. Lavender died in 1846 and George Farley in 1848. In December 1857 the bank failed, and John Gutch and John Owen, the surviving partners, became officially bankrupt. Although J. P. Lavender had been dead for several years his name appeared on some of the banknotes still in circulation at the time of the bankruptcy. To vindicate his memory, his daughter, Jane Lavender, provided funds to honour all such notes.

Jane Lavender and Mary Gutch donated the land and provided money for the building of St. Stephen's Church, Barbourne. Jane Lavender died in 1861 and Mary Gutch in 1873.

During the late 1820s and early 1830s William Oakey or Oakley was J. P. Lavender's tenant. James Smith was the next tenant followed by his son who also leased the butcher's shop on the corner of Butcher's Walk. After the son died his widow, Mary, took over the tenancy. In 1864 she alleged that the farm belonged to her and costs were incurred on the Lavender estate to prove that she did not. The farm was put up for sale by auction at The Talbot Inn, Worcester, on the 12th August 1864, and sold to a Mr. Goldinghouse of Ham for £1,220.

Halfway Cottage

In the 1930s and 1940s Halfway Cottage was a sweet shop kept by Mrs. Norkett.

The Cedars

In 1727 Joseph Weston of Worcester held the copyhold lease on 28 acres of land called Chapmans & Swynesland. He died in 1741 and bequeathed the farm to his daughter, Elizabeth Badeley the wife of William Badeley.

By 1831 the farm was in the hands of William Suttle of Hartlebury whose tenant was Thomas Trehearne. On William Suttle's death the farm passed to his son, Leonard, and after his death to his wife who held the farm for life then it passed to their son, Leonard William.

There was a dispute concerning Leonard Suttle's will in which it was alleged in 1852 that his attorney, Joseph Stallard, had interfered with the will, which he vehemently denied.

Joseph Fardon, a salt manufacturer of Droitwich, rented the property in 1861.

The farm was put up for sale in 1863 and purchased by William Broad Rowe, a nurseryman. The house was known then as Heath House, and it may have been William Broad Rowe who planted the cedar trees in the front garden. In 1867 the house and just over 6 acres of land was sold to James Baldwin of Stockport, Lancashire, for £2,850. He renamed the house, The Cedars. He disposed of the house and grounds in 1871 to Stiles Rich for £3,000.[13] Stiles Rich died in 1904 and The Cedars was sold and purchased by G. D. Hancock who sold it in 1912 probably to Captain Philip Vigors.

The Captain had had a distinguished army career having served in the South African War 1899-1902. He was mentioned in dispatches in 1901, in addition he received the MVO and five clasps and the King's Medal with two clasps.

At the outbreak of World War I he joined the Worcestershire Territorials and was appointed Adjutant. In December 1916 he was given a temporary appointment at the Command Depot at Sutton Coldfield, Warwickshire, where he was in charge of part of a recuperation camp. At the end of March 1917 he returned to Fernhill Heath for a short leave where he was taken ill and died suddenly at his home on the 2nd April.

A Military Funeral was held at Martin Hussingtree Church a few days later attended by family, friends, local residents and military staff from Sutton Coldfield. Six sergeants major bore the coffin on a wheeled bier from The Cedars to the church. The coffin was covered by a Union Jack and on the top were placed a number of wreaths. En route the Band of the 10th Royal Hussars played the 'Dead March' in 'Saul' and Chopin's 'Funeral March'. Following the church service interment took place in the churchyard after which all those present sang the National Anthem, followed by three volleys by the firing party of an officer and 21 men, and four buglers sounded the 'Last Post'.[14]

Captain Vigor's son was born in December 1917 and his widow, Gladys, remained at The Cedars. For many years she opened the garden to the

---

[13] *WRO. BA 4000/804 (i-v).*
[14] *Worcester Evening News & Times. 7th April 1917.*

The Cedars

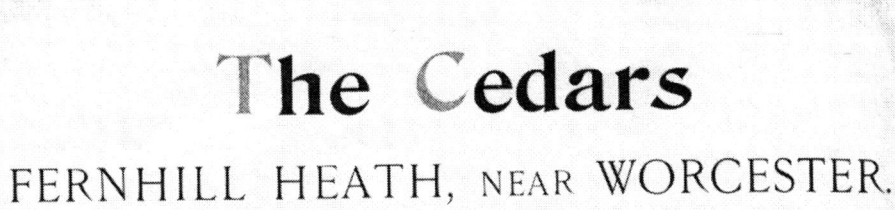

FERNHILL HEATH, NEAR WORCESTER.

A VALUABLE FREEHOLD RESIDENCE

TO BE SOLD BY AUCTION BY

Bentley, Hobbs & Mytton.

At the AUCTION MART,
WORCESTER.

On Saturday, 29th June, 1912
At 3 for 4 p.m.

Fig 76. The Cedars. Sale notice. 1912.

public under the National Gardens Scheme. In an interview with the Birmingham Evening Despatch in 1950 Mrs. Vigors said that during the past 80 years the house had grown to its present size, as more rooms were added.[22] Her son apparently inherited the house on marriage and Mrs. Vigors moved out to live elsewhere in the village. She died in 1967.

The house was sold to Roland Keene and following his death in 1961 the house remained empty and became derelict. A tramp got into the house and set fire to it and it was eventually demolished.

Fig 77. Demolition of The Cedars boundary wall.

The Cedars Sheltered Housing for the elderly was built in the grounds and was officially opened on the 14th March 1970 by the Chairman of Droitwich Rural District Council, Mr. J. R. Pointer. Several years later a two-storey wing was added on to the existing building. In the grounds only one cedar tree was left standing when the sheltered housing was built, and an attractive circular wooden seat placed around it. Soon afterwards the tree was felled, allegedly because it was diseased and unsafe, but it was found to be in good condition.

---

[15] *Birmingham Evening Despatch. 23rd June 1950.*

Fig 78. The Cedars, new sheltered housing for the elderly.
The cedar tree was felled allegedly diseased.

Old Cedars Cottage and Rammels Cottage

In 1875 Stiles Rich the owner of The Cedars purchased Old Cedars Cottage from Thomas Turner for £150.[16] The back garden belonging to the cottage was at the rear of where the Memorial Hall now stands and access to it was down the other side of the next-door cottage where the Rammel family lived. Both families had lived in the two cottages for many years. Eventually the Rammel family died out and the cottage came into the possession of Lord Hindlip. The cottage became derelict and was pulled down and the Memorial Hall was built on this site. The access road between the Memorial Hall and the hairdressers was once called Rammels Lane but the name has fallen into disuse.

---

[16] *WRO. BA 4000/804 (i-v).*

Fig 79. An early view of the village looking north.

Fernhill Heath War Memorial Hall

The Memorial Hall was opened in 1922 and became the venue for village social life. Dances were regularly held and all the family would go along for the evening. In the 1930s and up to the start of World War II there was an annual children's fancy dress dance with prizes. These dances were very popular and as many as 300 children sometimes attended.

On the 20th October 1950 Agatha, Lady Hindlip opened the Fernhill Heath Working Men's Club, this was a newly built extension at the rear of the Memorial Hall.

Over the years the Hall has been used for many social events, dancing, fund raising, school meals and school concerts, clubs and the pre-school Chatterbox play group. An annual Service of Remembrance, organised by the Memorial Hall Committee, is held in the Hall. In 1998 the hall was renamed the Fernhill Heath and District War Memorial Club.

Fig 80. Fernhill Heath War Memorial Hall. 1956.

Fig 81. Fernhill Heath Working Men's Dinner. c1950s.

Fernhill Heath Post Office

Henry Allsopp built this small cottage next to the Mission Room that opened in 1879. Small clay cross finials on the roof apex facing north and south give an indication that the cottage may have been used for some church purpose, perhaps a home for a Curate. Later the cottage became the post office and a shop and for a long time was run by the Barnett family. During the 1930s the local telephone exchange operated from here. The telephone numbers began with Fernhill Heath 1, Fernhill Heath 2 and so on. All telephone calls made went through the exchange. Sometimes there was a long wait either because the post office was busy or the family were in their living quarters behind the post office attending to their household chores.

The post office remained in the Hindlip Estate until 1962 when it was sold and became a ladies hairdressers' shop.

Fig 82. Fernhill Heath Post Office 1960.

Post Office Lane

The lane is in one of the oldest parts of the village. It takes its name from the old post office (now the hairdressers) opposite the lane.

Fig 83. Fernhill Heath Post Office. 1956.

Fig 84. Post Office Lane looking towards the Droitwich Road and Post Office. 1957. L – Rear of Pear Tree Cottage. R – Boundary wall of The Cedars with a rear view of hedge cutting in progress.

Fig 85. Outside the Post Office and looking across the Droitwich Road into Post Office Lane. 1957.

Fig 86. Post Office Lane looking towards the Droitwich Road and Hairdressers. 2007.

Fig 87. Outside the hair dressers (former Post Office) and looking across the Droitwich Road into Post Office Lane. 2007.

Fudgers

Opposite Hindlip School was the barber's shop with a tall red and white pole against the boundary hedge next to Pear Tree Cottage. Fred Purdy was the first barber, followed by Jim Lane and then George Fudger. The shop was demolished in 1968.

Fig 88. G. Fudger, Hairdresser. 1956.

Woodbine Cottage

The cottage was situated between the barber's shop and the gardener's cottage (Fernhill Heath Cottage). Woodbine Cottage was demolished around 1963.

Fig 89. Woodbine Cottage 1956.

Henry Allsopp's houses, 57-63 Droitwich Road

The land can be traced back to the old bowling green belonging to the 18th century 'Bull Inn'. Later two pairs of semi-detached cottages were built on the former bowling green and were included in the sale of Fearnall Heath House in 1825. In 1867 Henry Allsopp purchased the cottages, demolished them, and built these two pairs of semi-detached houses for his estate workers. The houses were called, The Poplars, The Elms, The Laurels and The Hollies.

Following the opening of Hindlip School in the former Mission Room, Number 63, The Poplars, became the Headmaster's home. At the beginning of the 20th century Number 57, then The Hollies, the house nearest to the school, was occupied by the 3rd Lord Hindlip's chef, and soon afterwards became the village Police House for many years. Upon the appointment of Vernon Hedges as Headmaster in 1946 the village policeman moved to a purpose-built house south of the village next to the car showroom, Fernhill Heath Motors (now part of Stoneycroft Close), and

Vernon Hedges moved into Rosedene, formerly The Hollies, until his retirement. The houses were sold in 1962 as part of the Hindlip Estate.

In August 2000 Mrs. Helen Hadley of The Laurels celebrated her 100th birthday with a family party.

Fig 90. The Hollies (Rosedene), Hindlip School and Fernhill Heath Post Office. c1930.

Fernhill Heath House

In January 1803 Thomas Weston opened Fearnall Heath House as a school for young gentlemen. He died soon afterwards. In 1825 the House, several cottages and the Bull meadows were sold to James Williams, an army surgeon. He died in 1845 and left this small estate to his brother, George, the Rector of Martin Hussingtree. George died in 1852 and his two nephews, The Revd George Williams of Minchinhampton, Gloucestershire, and John Williams, inherited the estate and sold it to Francis Needham, a partner in the company of Needham & Walker, which traded at Lowesmoor Wharf, Diglis Basin and the Worcester Corn Exchange. Francis Needham died in 1867 and Henry Allsopp purchased the property and leased it out to various tenants who were all connected with the Worcestershire Hunt.

ANOTHER BLOCK OF BUILDINGS with separate driving way approach, consists of Coach House, Loose Box, Shed, and Two Pigstyes.

The Grounds comprise first rate walled-in Kitchen Garden, Lawns, and Shrubberies, and Two Pieces of Excellent Pasture Land.

The Property is situate in a good HUNTING and RESIDENTIAL LOCALITY, and easy of access from London, Birmingham, and the North, being close to FERNHILL HEATH STATION, on main Birmingham, Worcester, and London Line, and midway between the CITY OF WORCESTER and DROITWICH.

It is near the Worcestershire Hunt Kennels, and the meets of the Worcestershire and Croome Hounds are within easy distance.

VIEW OF FERNHILL HEATH HOUSE.

Fig 91. Fernhill Heath House. 1912.

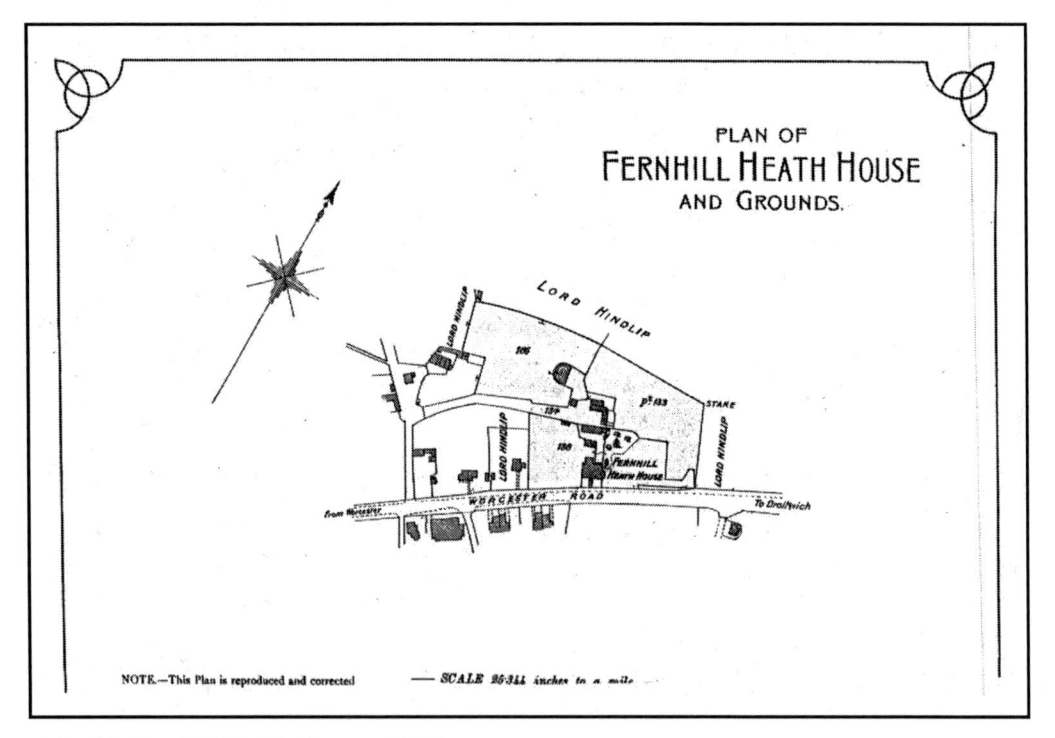

Fig 92. Fernhill Heath House. 1912.

In 1881 a London solicitor, William P. Hughes, resided there, and who later moved to Morton House.[17]

John Oswald Trotter was appointed Field Master in 1896, and after his marriage to Sophia Fenwick in January 1898 they moved into Fernhill Heath House. Whist out hunting he was injured in a fall and before he could get up his horse had trodden on his chest. He died on the 21st February and was buried in Martin Hussingtree churchyard. The next tenant was Frederick W. Morton, Field Master, and his family who resided there until 1912 when the 3rd Lord Hindlip put the house and land together with Martin Hall Farm in Martin Hussingtree for sale. The sale notice described Fernhill Heath House as a 'hunting box'.[18] The house was withdrawn from sale at £900 and remained in the Hindlip family and continued to be leased out to various tenants. In 1925 Mrs. Mildred Berkeley moved into the House. She began to take an interest in the village and started a Brotherhood and a Mothers' Meeting group. At Christmas these groups and the pupils of Hindlip School were entertained

---

[17] 1881 Census.
[18] WRO. 4925/60.

separately to tea in the hut in the House grounds. She died in 1944. After World War II, Agatha, Lady Hindlip moved to Fernhill Heath House and lived there until her death in 1962.

Sandyway

Although Sandyway is some distance away from the village itself it has played an important part throughout the history of Fernhill Heath. Here the Martin Brook is the boundary of the civil parish of North Claines and the two ecclesiastical parishes of Hindlip and Martin Hussingtree. The two cottages, formerly Hindlip School, have the odd distinction of being situated in the civil parish of North Claines, the ecclesiastical parish of Hindlip and their postal address is in Martin Hussingtree!

Sandyway is either the first approach to Fernhill Heath or the last away from a village whose residents have always had its best interests at heart.

Fig 93. Sandyway. 2007.

Image References

Chapter 1.
Fig 1. Map of Tapenhall. Reproduced by permission of Ordnance Survey on behalf of HMSO. © Copyright 1997. All rights reserved. Ordnance Survey Licence No. 100047130.
Fig 2. Ecclesiastical Parish boundaries 1895. Reproduced by permission of Ordnance Survey on behalf of HMSO. © Copyright 1905. All rights reserved. Ordnance Survey Licence No. 100047130.
Fig 3. North Claines Civil Parish Boundary 1987. Reproduced by permission of Ordnance Survey on behalf of HMSO. © Crown Copyright 1997. All rights reserved. Ordnance Survey Licence No. 100047130.

Chapter 2.
Fig 4. Vernal Heath 1751-1753. John Doharty, Jnr. 1751-53. Reproduced by permission of Worcestershire Record Office. WRO. BA 3634/48. (vi) 43969.
Fig 5. The former carriage drive to Hindlip House. G. M. Lawley.
Fig 6. 16th Century Hindlip House. Loaned by Salwarpe, Hindlip & Martin Hussingtree PCC.
Fig 7. Sketch of 'The Bull Inn' and Bowling Green. BA 2636/47674.
Fig 8. Widefield and Perry-field open strips. John Doharty, Jnr. 1751-53. Reproduced by permission of Worcestershire Record Office. WRO. BA 3634/48. (vi) 43969.
Fig 9. Wall Tablet in Pebworth church. G. M. Lawley.
Fig 10. Encroachments 1798. WRO. BA 2636. 47668.
Fig 11. The Lodge 2007. G. Lawley.
Fig 12. Carriage Drive 2007. G. Lawley.

Chapter 3.
Fig 13. Claines Tithe Map. 1840. WRO. BA 3587/7.
Fig 14. The Wheatfield formerly the Widefield. WRO. BA 3587/7.
Fig 15. Claines Tithe Map 1840. WRO. BA 3587/7.
Fig 16. Fernhill Heath Station. Loaned by Malcolm Nixon.
Fig 17. Fernhill Heath Station. Loaned by Malcolm Nixon.
Fig 18. 1854 Railway Timetable. Worcester Journal. 1854.
Fig 19. Henry Allsopp's houses. 1956. Mrs. W. R. Young.

Chapter 4.
Fig 20. Foundation stone, Baptist Chapel. G. Lawley.
Fig 21. Baptist Chapel Concert 1914. Berrow's Worcester Journal Supplement. 21st March 1914.
Fig 22. Road widening on Red Hill. 1913. County Surveyor.
Fig 23. Road widening on Red Hill. 1913. County Surveyor.
Fig 24. Roll of Honour, Fernhill Heath War Memorial. Bob Rosier.
Fig 25. Roll of Honour, Fernhill Heath War Memorial. Bob Rosier.
Fig 26. Mrs. Dorothy Wilde and friends of the Half Way Public House. Unknown.
Fig 27. Danes Green Farm. Sale and Plan. 1918. WRO. BA 5589/90. (i), (ii), (iii).
Fig 28. Road widening on Rose Bank and house building in progress. 1938. County Surveyor.

Chapter 4 *cont.*
Fig 29. Hindlip, Martin Hussingtree and Fernhill Heath residents outside Hindlip Stables. 1937. Loaned by Margaret Payton.
Fig 30. Advertisement for Coronation of King George VI. WRO. BA 3039.
Fig 31. Fernhill Heath Home Guard. Worcester Evening News & Times.
Fig 32. Dilmore Cottages 1952. Mrs. W. R. Young.

Chapter 5.
Fig 33. Eileen Mann, Hindlip School Coronation Queen. 1953. Loaned by Eileen Williams.
Fig 34. Signal box and new footbridge. Worcester Evening News & Times.
Fig 35. Preston's Garage sold on the 18th July 1988 for re-development. Loaned by Phyllis Byatt.

Chapter 6.
Fig 36. Thatch Cottage. G. Lawley.
Fig 37. The former Workhouse, Droitwich Road. G. M. Lawley.

Chapter 7.
Fig 38. Hindlip School. c1902. Hindlip C.E. First School.
Fig 39. The Overseas Club. 1915. Colin Cook.
Fig 40. Empire Day. 1916. Colin Cook.
Fig 41. Hindlip School. 1956. Mrs. W. R. Young.
Fig 42. New extension. 1989. Hindlip C.E. First School.
Fig 43. New extension. 1989. Hindlip C.E. First School.

Chapter 8.
Fig 44. Sale of Oakfield. 1855. Worcester Herald 18th August 1855.
Fig 45. Women's Land Army at Oakfield House. The River School.
Fig 46. Oakfield Lodge. 1952. Mrs. W. R. Young.
Fig 47. Morton House Estate Sale. 1930. WRO. BA 5240/3b.
Fig 48. Dilmore Lodge. c1900. W.R.O.
Fig 49. Pear Tree House. 1952. Mrs. W. R. Young.
Fig 50. The Forge. 1952. Mrs. W. R. Young.
Fig 51. Tapenhall House sale notice. 1935. WRO. BA 5240/46.
Fig 52. Fernhill Heath Fete 1909. Berrow's Worcester Journal Supplement. 12th June 1909.
Fig 53. Fernhill Heath and Hindlip Mothers' Meeting excursion. 1910. Berrow's Worcester Journal Supplement. 25th June 1910.
Fig 54. The old piggeries and slaughterhouse. G. M. Lawley.
Fig 55. L-R. Preston's Garage, 'White Hart Hotel', the railway cottage and 'Bull Hotel'. c. late 1930s. County Surveyor.
Fig 56. Preston's Garage. Loaned by Phyllis Byatt.
Fig 57. Bull Inn. Mrs. W. R. Young.
Fig 58. Brenda Baylis outside her father's shop, G. S. Baylis, Baker & Confectioner. Loaned by Brenda Baylis.
Fig 59. Grocery prices in December 1905. Loaned by Brenda Baylis.
Fig 60. George Baylis with his white hooded delivery carts. Loaned by Brenda Baylis.

Fig 61. George Baylis. The proud owner of a new delivery van. Loaned by Brenda Baylis.
Fig 62. Edgar Davis Antiques. 1985. The Trumpet.
Fig 63. High Barn (Formerly The Laurels). D. Clifford.
Fig 64. Sale notice. The Laurels. 1866. Berrow's Worcester Journal.
Fig 65. Byre Cottage, Ivy Lane. c1970. Worcestershire County Council.
Fig 66. The Live And Let Live. Loaned by Joyce Eden.
Fig 67. The 'Live and Let Live' public house built in the late 1930s. Worcester Evening News & Times.
Fig 68. Staymore Café. 1954. Mrs. W. R. Young.
Fig 69. Sale notice. 1944. Loaned by Bill Toppin.
Fig 70. The Stores. 1954. Mrs. W. R. Young.
Fig 71. Local businesses and public houses in 1985. The Trumpet.
Fig 72. Lilac Cottage. 1954. Mrs. W. R. Young.
Fig 73. The 'Half Way House'. 1954. Mrs. W. R. Young.
Fig 74. Drug Stores. 1954. Mrs. W. R. Young.
Fig 75. Fernhill Heath Baptist Chapel. 1954. Mrs. W. R. Young.
Fig 76. The Cedars. Sale notice. 1912. WRO. BA 5240/2.
Fig 77. Demolition of The Cedars boundary wall. Worcestershire County Council.
Fig 78. The Cedars, new sheltered housing for the elderly. Worcester Evening News & Times.
Fig 79. An early view of the village looking north. County Surveyor.
Fig 80. Fernhill Heath War Memorial Hall. 1956. Mrs. W. R. Young.
Fig 81. Fernhill Heath Working Men's Dinner. c1950s. Fernhill Heath Working Men's Club.
Fig 82. Fernhill Heath Post Office 1960. B. Buckle.
Fig 83. Fernhill Heath Post Office. 1956. Mrs. W. R. Young.
Fig 84. Post Office Lane looking towards the Droitwich Road and Post Office. 1957. County Surveyor.
Fig 85. Outside the Post Office and looking across the Droitwich Road into Post Office Lane. 1957. County Surveyor.
Fig 86. Post Office Lane looking towards the Droitwich Road and Hairdressers. 2007. G. Lawley.
Fig 87. Outside the Hairdressers (former Post Office) and looking across the Droitwich Road into Post OfficeLane. 2007. G. Lawley.
Fig 88. G. Fudger, Hairdresser. 1956. Mrs. W. R. Young.
Fig 89. Woodbine Cottage 1956. Mrs. W. R. Young.
Fig 90. The Hollies (Rosedene), Hindlip School and Fernhill Heath Post Office. c1930. County Surveyor
Fig 91. Fernhill Heath House. 1912. WRO. BA 5240/2.
Fig 92. Fernhill Heath House. 1912. WRO. BA 5240/2.
Fig 93. Sandyway. 2007. G. M. Lawley

Index

Allsopp, Henry 36, 37,105, 146, 151, 152
Allsopp, MP, The Hon. Samuel Charles 37
Ashton, Mrs. M. L. 109
Assembly room 70
Astwood 5, 7, 8

Badeley, Elizabeth 139
Badeley, William 139
Baldwin, James 140
Barneby, Thomas 109
Barneby, William 109
Barnett family 146
Barton, Miss 101
Baylis, Brenda 123
Baylis, George Hunt 123
Baylis, George Spencer 123
Baylis, Richard 113
Benton, John 18, 19, 20
Benton, Mary 18, 19
Berkeley, Catherine 22
Berkeley, Jane 22
Berkeley, John 22
Berkeley, Mildred 97, 99, 154
Berkeley, Mrs. 98, 99
Beverburn 5
Bevere 5, 7, 8
Bevereye 5
Blackpole Road 63, 72
Blacksmith, Vernal Heath 31
Blake, John 88
Bombing raid 62
Bough, Caroline 119
Brazier Ltd, J. & A. 53
Briary Fields 14
Broadfield Crescent 17
Broom Meadow Road 71
Broom, The 2, 60
Brum, The 55, 60, 70, 74, 75, 102, 117, 119
Bull Meadows 15, 22, 152
Burcher, Mr. 114
Burt, John 84
Butchers Walk 28, 130
Byre, The 128

Cadbury Brothers 44, 60, 61, 62
Carden, Henry 107
Carr, Bob 61
Cartwright, John 88

Cedars, The 17, 26, 63, 73, 74, 139, 140, 141, 142, 143, 148
Cedars The, Sheltered Housing 142
Chapmans & Swynesland 139
Chatley 3
Chichester, Col. 51, 99
Civil Defence Headquarters 112
Claines
Claines ,1, 2, 4, 5, 6, 7, 8, 10, 12, 13, 17, 19, 20, 38, 41, 45, 57, 60, 61, 63, 71, 81, 82, 83, 84, 85, 87, 90, 94, 97, 98, 99, 100, 102, 105, 107, 109, 115, 117, 119, 123, 127, 138, 139, 155
Claines and Whistones 6, 17
Claines Church 2, 4, 5, 6, 7, 8, 81, 82, 84, 107, 117, 138
Claines Churchwardens 105
Claines Churchyard 8, 45, 82, 83
Claines Civil Parish Boundary 10
Claines, Hollow or Holy 5
Claines Lane 2, 8, 57, 60, 87, 107
Claines School 71, 94, 97
Claines United Charity 6
Claines Vestry 6, 35, 41, 81-90
Clifton Villa 117
Clinton, George 123
Community Centre 71, 75
Compton, Jane 22
Compton, Sir William 14, 22
Congregational Church 29
Cook, Colin 123
Cooke, James Cooper 112
Copple, Mary 127
Copple, William 127
Copson, John 83
Copsons Land 28
Copyhold and Freehold land 12, 18, 105
Cornmeadow Lane 8, 39, 60, 62, 71
Coronation, King Edward VII 95
Coronation, King George VI 57, 58
Coronation, Queen Elizabeth II 68
Cottage, Woodbine 150, 151
County Council, Hereford & Worcester 74, 75, 78, 102
County Council, Worcestershire 7, 8, 55, 71, 95, 107, 109
Crescent, Broadfield 71
Cresswell Close 71, 117

Cresswell, James 71
Crowle 85, 88

Danes Green 18, 20, 25, 51, 60, 81, 117, 130
Danes Green Farm 51, 52, 53, 63, 78, 79, 117
Davey, Joseph 93
Davidson, William 107
Deal Cottage 128
Deans Green 18, 25, 81, 117
Deans Green Farm 18, 20, 117
Diamond Jubilee, Queen Victoria 39
Dilmore
Dillmoor 2, 3, 11, 12, 18
Dilmore 3, 11, 18, 25, 29, 31, 60, 64, 67, 71, 74
Dillmoor, Great 12, 18
Dilmore Avenue 8, 64, 71, 75
Dilmore Cottage 61, 105, 112, 113
Dilmore Cottages 61, 64, 65
Dilmore House 31, 105, 113
Dilmore House Hotel 21
Dilmore Lane 11, 12, 18, 20, 28, 31, 51, 53, 54, 60, 61, 64, 74, 78, 113, 117
Dilmore Lodge 31, 60, 113, 114
Dobbs, William 90
Domesday Book 5
Downes, John 113
Droitwich 1, 5, 8, 11, 15, 16, 17, 44, 51, 55, 64, 67, 70, 72, 78, 90, 98, 99, 100, 101, 123, 140
Droitwich Road 3, 8, 28, 32, 38, 44, 45, 53, 54, 61, 64, 67, 73, 77, 78, 79, 84, 90, 107, 109, 117, 121, 148, 149, 151
Droitwich Rural District Council 7, 53, 55, 56, 70, 71, 73, 142
Droitwich Rural Tribunal 97
Droitwich Union Workhouse 90

Eastfield Close 71
Ecclesiastical parish boundaries 1, 9
Elbury Hill 2
Elm Cottage 112, 113
Ely, John 89
Emuss, John 130
Encroachments 21
Everall, Elizabeth 88

Fardon, Joseph 140

Farley, Harry 56, 129
Fernhill Heath
Fearnal 2
Fearnall 2, 22
Fernhull 2, 5
Ffournall 2
Fournall 2
Fearnal Heath 22
Fearnall Heath 2, 6, 7, 22, 25, 26, 29, 32, 34, 35, 36, 38, 84, 85, 86, 87, 88, 89, 90, 116
Vernal 2
Vernal Heath 2, 11, 12, 13, 16, 17, 18, 20, 25, 82, 127
Fearnall Heath Brickyard 38
Fearnall Heath District Farmers' Society, The 35
Fearnall/ Fernhill Heath House 22, 26, 35, 36, 151, 152
Fearnall Heath Workhouse 6, 25, 26, 28, 29, 88, 120, 130, 136, 139
Fernhill Heath Baptist Chapel 41, 42, 68, 137, 138
Fernhill Heath House 15, 38, 61, 63, 72, 74, 78
Fernhill Heath Motors 151
Fernhill Heath Post Office 146, 147, 152
Fernhill Heath Railway Station 34, 75
Fernhill Heath War Memorial Hall 44, 45, 61, 64, 68, 70, 73, 74, 79, 98, 99, 143, 144, 145
Fernhill Heath Working Men's Club 144
Finch, William 113
Fir Tree Road 74
Firlands Close 71
Franks, Richard 117
Freeman, Joseph 84
Fudger, George 150

Gascoigne, F. O. 45
Goodwood Close 8, 75
Goodwood Green development 75
Goodwood House 8, 117
Gough, The Revd Arthur 127
Grange, The 3, 20, 51, 63, 99, 105, 109
Gravel pits 86
Great Western Railway 32
Green Belt 79
Green Lane 2
Green Way 1
Green Weg 1
Green, William 85

Guit Stocking fields 28
Gutch, John Mathew 89, 138
Gutch, John 139
Gutch, Mary 138, 139

Haden, Henry 116
Hadley, Helen 152
Hancock, G. D. 140
Harcourt, Edward 16
Harrison, Robert 20
Hawford House 3
Hawkes, Mr. 101
Heath House 105, 117, 140
Heath Side 119
Heather Moor 2
Heddon House 113, 114
Hedges, Vernon 99, 151, 152
Hemming, P. C. 129
Henney, Sarah 129
Highways Acts 11, 12
Hill, Revd H. W. 8
Hill, William 14
Himbleton 85, 88
Hindlip 1, 5, 6, 7, 8, 9, 17, 28, 36, 37, 38, 44, 45, 57, 61, 62, 68, 88, 94, 98, 100, 119, 155
Hindlip Estate 22, 36, 38, 72, 90, 100, 146, 152
Hindlip Hall 28, 36, 61, 70, 94, 112
Hindlip House 14, 15, 22, 26, 36
Hindlip Lane 11, 60, 63, 72
Hindlip Lodge 1, 55, 73
Hindlip Park 1, 3, 6, 14, 68
Hindlip School 7, 36, 41, 44, 45, 67, 68, 69, 70, 72, 74, 75, 93, 95, 98, 100, 101, 102, 150, 151, 152, 154, 155
Hindlip Stables 57
Hindlip, Lord 37
Hindlip, 2nd Lord 38, 94
Hindlip, 3rd Lord 8, 38, 44, 53, 60, 90, 95, 98, 151, 154
Hindlip, 4th Lord 74
Hindlip, Agatha, Lady 37, 60, 61, 70, 72, 79, 144, 155
Hindlip, Lady 2
Hirons, F. M. 100
Holden, Julia 112
Holmes, Mary Catherine Bell 128
Hope, Nellie 131
Hughes, William Price 109
Hundred of Oswaldslow 5

Hurst Farm 12, 17, 38, 62, 63, 72
Hurst Ground, The 17
Hurst Lane 3, 12, 13, 36, 38, 53, 60, 63, 72, 76, 78, 120
Hurst, The 2, 17

Ivy Lane 12, 13, 28, 71, 79, 128, 137

Jeffrey, George 121
Jew, John 18, 113
Jolley Charity, Susannah 117
Jolley, Annie 117, 137
Jolley, Susannah 90, 117

Kennels Lane 8, 17, 64, 71, 77, 78
Lady Huntingdon's Chapel 31
Lane House 71
Lane, James 71
Lane, Jim 150
Larkworthy, Mrs. 41
Laurels, The (High Barn) 127, 128, 151, 152
Lavender, Jane 139
Lavender, John Pearkes 138, 139
Lay Subsidy Rolls 5
Lightband, Richard 114
Lightband, Richard the younger 114
Linacres Farm 3
Ling Meadow 2
Links Lane 12, 17, 27, 36, 38
Lloyd, John 14
Local Education Authority 70, 93
Locke, Alexander 41
Lower Saltway 1
Lower Town 12, 17, 78, 130
Lowesmoor 1, 152
Lucy, Ann 89
Lucy, Benjamin 89
Lucy, William 89

Manor of Claines 6, 12, 13, 25
Manorial Court Baron 20
Manorial Court Rolls 11
Marmont, Mary 29, 105, 115
Martin Brook 1, 3, 4, 6, 8, 12, 15, 56, 155
Martin Hussingtree 1, 3, 8, 9, 12, 17, 22, 36, 38, 45, 57, 61, 68, 72, 85, 88, 97, 98, 99, 100, 119, 152, 154, 155
Martin Hussingtree Church 97, 99, 140, 154
Martin, W. A. 115
Meadows, The 71

Mence, John 115
Midland Bank 126
Midland Red Omnibus Co. Ltd. 44
Mildenham Mill 3
Mildenham with Hawford 5, 7
Milnham with Hayford 5
Miller, Olive 60, 117
Ministry of Defence 61, 112
Mission Room 7, 17, 36, 95, 146, 151
Moors, The 2
Morris, Henry Bradley 127
Henry Morris 127
Morris, Susannah Ann 127
Morris, Thomas 16
Morton Avenue 53, 55, 64
Morton House 21, 38, 53, 61, 109, 111, 112, 154
Morton House Estate 53, 111
Morton Road 53, 55
Morton, Frederick W. 154
Mull/Mulls family 4
Mytton, Herbert 90
Mytton, Hubert 120, 136
Mytton, H. 134
Mytton, Jack 90, 120

National Farm Survey 63
Needham, Francis 152
North Claines Parish Council 38, 39
Northern Link, A449 1, 8, 67
Northfield Close 74
Northwick 5, 6, 7, 8, 38
Northwick, New 60

O'Keys Lane 28, 35, 41, 137
Oakey, William 139
Oakeys Farm 17
Oakfield Academy 41, 105, 115
Oakfield House 2, 3, 29, 61, 63, 100, 105, 107, 108, 109
Oakfield Lodge 105, 109, 110
Oddingley 2
Old brickyard 53, 60
Old Cedars Cottage 143
Ombersley 2, 3, 41, 87
Ombersley Road 38, 72, 84
Ombersley Roads 11
Overseers of the Poor 6, 81, 83, 86
Oxford, Worcester and Wolverhampton Railway 2, 32, 34

Partridge, Elizabeth 112, 113
Partridge ,Hannah 112
Partridge, John 21, 112
Partridge, John Jnr, 112
Partridge, Sarah 112
Pear Tree Cottage 148, 150
Pear Tree House 31, 51, 54, 114, 115
Pear Tree at Smite 38
Pebworth church 19
Pelican crossing 73
Perdiswell 8, 25, 55, 60
Perdiswell Estate 38, 109
Perry Croft 20, 28
Perrycroft Close 8, 17, 71, 90
Pershore Lane 2, 57, 72
Pidcock, Henry 107
Pinkett, Frederick 113
Pinkett, Thomas Buckle 113
Pitchcroft 39
Port Straet 3
Porter family, The 4
Porter, George 4
Porter, John 4
Porters Mill 3, 4, 12
Post Office Lane 12, 17, 28, 60, 73, 74, 75, 78, 79, 97, 146, 148, 149
Potter, William 114
Pound, The 31
Preston Court 71
Preston, Mr 121
Priddey, Joseph 16
Prosser, William 114
Public Inquiry 74, 79
Public Houses
Bull Inn 15, 16, 32, 57, 122, 151
Bull Inn bowling green 70, 151
Durham Ox, The 32, 122
Half Way House 32, 45, 55, 136
Hop Pole 28
Live and Let Live 28, 70, 78, 79, 89, 129, 130
Old House at Home, The 31, 115, 116
Plough Inn, The 28, 89
White Hart, The 28, 29, 32, 38, 68, 70

Puck Pit 20, 25, 51, 83, 109
Pulpit 20, 25, 51
Purdy, Fred 150

Queen Victoria's Golden Jubilee 94

Railway Accident 67
Rainbow Hill 1, 7
Rammels Cottage 143
Rammels Lane 143
Rector 152
Red Hill 11, 12, 18, 20, 21, 43, 53, 116
Reynolds, Charles 17, 20, 138
Reynolds, George 17
Rich, Stiles 140, 143
River Salwarpe 3, 6
River School, The 2, 105, 109
River Severn 1, 5, 6, 38
Rosedene 152
Rose Bank 1, 2, 11, 53, 54, 60, 61, 105, 117
Rose Mount 53
Ross, John 117
Ross, Margaret 117
Rowe, William Broad 140
Russell, Luke 85

Salt Lane 1, 6
Salwarpe 3, 6, 12, 85, 88, 119
Sandyway 1, 3, 4, 6, 7, 8, 14, 15, 22, 29, 36, 56, 68, 93, 105, 155
Sewage & Water Scheme 55, 56
Shepherd Pte, George 97
Shrawley Charity 20
Shrawley Road 17, 20, 71, 75
Silver Jubilee of King George V 57
Sling Lane 12, 28, 68, 123, 125
Smite 5, 6, 7, 38
Smite Farm 8, 25
Smite Hill 7, 8
Smith, James 139
Smith, James Jnr 139
Smith, Mary 139
Smith, William 14
South Wales & Cannock Chase Coal Company 34
Southwell, Lord 22, 36
Speed limit 55, 62, 73
Spellis 1, 7, 17, 56, 119
Spellis Farm 8, 13, 17, 35, 38, 62, 63, 72
Spellis Fields 8
Spellis Green 11, 12, 62, 63, 72
Springfield House 109
St. Helen's Church, Worcester 5
Stallard, Joseph 140

Station Road 3, 8, 12, 17, 20, 38, 51, 53, 54, 56, 60, 64, 71, 74, 77, 78, 79, 112, 130
Staymore Café 131
Stezaker, Mrs. 131
Stores,The Central 134
Stores, The 134, 136
Stubby Furlong 2
Styles, Thomas 97
Sugar and Seg Mead 2
Super Shop 137
Surman, William 16
Suttle, Leonard William 139
Suttle, William 139

Tapenhall
Tapenhall 3, 4, 5, 7, 12, 63, 64, 81, 83
Tapenhall Farm 51, 70
Tapenhall Farm in Ombersley 3
Tapenhall House 3, 31, 60, 90, 117, 118
Tapenhall Road 3, 64
Upper Tapenhall 20, 60, 63
Upper Tapenhall Farm 3, 63
Taylor, William 14, 130
Teare, Horace 95, 97, 98
Teare, Mrs. 97
Tetnal 2
Thomas, Ernest Percy (Pumpy Thomas) 117
Thompson, George 88
Thorneycroft 31, 114
Three Counties Agricultural Society 68
Tibberton 85, 88, 100
Timms, Edwin 127
Tithe Commutation Act 1836 25
Tolladine 5, 7, 8
Tollerdine 5
Tolwardine 5
Tootenhall 2
Trehearne, Thomas 139
Trotter, John Oswald 154
Tuffley 115
Tuffley, Benjamin 115
Turner, John 117
Turnpike, Worcester to Bromsgrove 11
Tutnall 2, 19, 81
Tutnall House 2, 57
Tyler, Harry 98

Vigors, Emily 51
Vigors, Gladys 140
Vigors, Philip 140

Wake Sundays 35
Wakeman family 25
Walker, Mary 19, 81, 82
Wall, William 87, 88
Warndon 6, 7, 8, 72, 85, 88
Weights and Measures 112
Weston, Joseph 17, 139
Weston, T. 22, 49
Weston, Thomas 152
Wheatfield 25, 27, 32, 38
Wheatfield Villa 38
Wheeler, J. A. 94, 95
Whistones 5, 6, 17
White, Henry 115, 116
White, Joseph 39, 115
White, Henry Jnr 116
Wich Road 11, 12, 13, 14, 20, 130
Wich-Way Close 28
Widefield 12, 15, 17, 18, 20, 25, 27, 32, 38
Wilde, Dorothy 45, 50
Williams, James 22, 152
Williams, John 152
Williams, Joseph 113
Williams, The Revd George of Martin Hussingtree 22
Williams, The Revd George of Minchinhampton 152
Wilson, Catherine 107
Wilson, The Revd Joseph Bowstead 107
Windmill Cottages 117
Windyridge 117
Women's Land Army 44, 61, 107, 108
Woodbine Cottage 150
Woodfields 2
Wooldridge, John 97
Worcester 1, 2, 3, 4, 5, 7, 8, 11, 15, 17, 25, 29, 32, 34, 36, 38, 44, 45, 51, 53, 54, 55, 60, 61, 67, 68, 70, 72, 75, 81, 83, 84, 86, 87, 90, 94, 98, 102, 112, 113, 123, 129, 138, 139
Worcester City Council 1, 71
Worcester County Council 8
Worcester Diocesan Education Board 93
Worcester Tramways 44
Worcestershire Hunt 8, 17, 36, 37, 63, 152
Worcestershire War Agricultural Committee 44
Workhouse 81, 82, 84, 85, 86, 87, 88, 89, 90
Worrall, John 117
Worrall, John Jnr, 117

Worrall, Susannah 117
Wyatt, George 45
Wychavon District Council 1, 10
Wychavon District Council's Local Plan 78
Wynne, Miss 99

Yeoman, Mr. 81, 82